D0948116

Twayne's English Authors Series

EDITOR OF THIS VOLUME

Sarah W. R. Smith

Tufts University

Robert Bage

TEAS 249

ROBERT BAGE

By Peter Faulkner

University of Exeter

TWAYNE PUBLISHERS
A DIVISION OF G. K. HALL & CO., BOSTON

Published in 1979 by Twayne Publishers,
A Division of G. K. Hall & Co.
All Rights Reserved

Printed on permanent/durable acid-free paper and bound
in the United States of America

First Printing

Library of Congress Cataloging in Publication Data

Faulkner, Peter.
Robert Bage.

(Twaynes English authors series ; TEAS 249)
Bibliography: p. 174-78
Includes index.
1.   Bage, Robert, 1728-1801 — Criticism and
interpretation.   I.   Title
PR4049.B5Z69   823'.6   78-14273
ISBN 0-8057-6739-8

Contents

About the Author

Peter Faulkner gained First Class Honours in English at the University of Cambridge, and an MA from Birmingham for a thesis on the Literary Criticism of W. B. Yeats. He taught at Fircroft College, Birmingham, the University of Durham and Fourah Bay College, Freetown, Sierra Leone, and is now a Senior Lecturer in English at the University of Exeter.

His publications include: *William Morris and W. B. Yeats, William Morris: The Critical Heritage,* editions of Carlyle's letters to Thomas Redwood and of Thomas Holcroft's *Anna St. Ives,* and more recently, books on *Modernism* and *Humanism in the English Novel.*

Preface

In late eighteenth-century England many important social and political issues became very acute, and were widely discussed in various forms of literature and journalism. The debate on the French Revolution may be taken as the most dramatic and significant of these controversies, but it was only a part of that wider discussion of the form society should take which marks the whole period from the American War of Independence onwards. As England developed and changed away from its feudal and agrarian past into the unknown modern world, a large number of fundamental issues were articulated and discussed. Notable contributions to these discussions came from Edmund Burke on the conservative side, and such thinkers and controversialists as William Godwin, Thomas Paine, and Mary Wollstonecraft on the radical side. The latter were united in their belief in free enquiry and the rights of man, ideas which if accepted would accelerate the whole process of social change that technical and industrial developments were already causing.

The period was not a distinguished one in the history of the English novel, but it did produce two types of novel worthy of critical consideration. On the one hand Gothic fiction developed its peculiar and influential form of Romanticism, while on the other a number of writers used the novel as a deliberate contribution to the war of ideas. Godwin himself wrote *Caleb Williams, or Things as They Are* in 1794, reinforcing in fiction the arguments of his *Enquiry Concerning Political Justice* of 1793 (though also introducing a quite different kind of emotional intensity), and was supported by such other radicals as Thomas Holcroft, in *Anna St. Ives* (1792) and *Hugh Trevor* (1794–97). But in some ways the most interesting, and certainly the most entertaining, contributions on the radical side came from the little-known Staffordshire papermaker Robert Bage, whose six novels published between 1782 and 1796 express a radical point of view with a relaxed wit which is unusual in controversial areas.

The aim of the present book is to draw attention to Bage's little-known novels, and to show their relationship to the age in which they were written. The first chapter focuses on Bage's life, quoting extensively from his letters preserved in the Birmingham Public Library (to which institution I am particularly grateful). Only a few of these letters have been published previously, so that they are a new primary source for understanding Bage in his time and place, a working middle-class man in the Birmingham district, well aware of the developments of that area of England during the early Industrial Revolution. The book then proceeds to a chronological examination of Bage's six novels, relating each of them to its concern with important ideas of the time. The first four, *Mount Henneth* (1782), *Barham Downs* (1784), *The Fair Syrian* (1787), and *James Wallace* (1788), are shown to be interesting for their ideas and the humor with which they are expressed, but the highest claims are made for Bage's last two novels, *Man as He Is* (1792) and *Hermsprong, or Man as He Is Not* (1796). In these, it is suggested, the political and social issues of the day are explored from the standpoint of an intelligent and good-humored Radicalism, which makes them attractive in their own right and perhaps carries a message for our own times.

The book ends with a consideration of Bage's reputation, and the evidence of early nineteenth-century taste provided by Walter Scott's criticisms of Bage in 1824; of his contribution to the novel of ideas, including his relationship to such better-known later practitioners as Thomas Love Peacock; and of recent views of his novels.

I should like to express my thanks to all those who have encouraged my interest in Bage, including Professor T. J. B. Spencer, Professor R. Sharrock, Professor T. S. Dorsch, and my wife, Pamela, and to the secretarial staff of Exeter University Department of English for their efforts with the manuscript.

PETER FAULKNER

Universtiy of Exeter

Chronology

1728 Robert Bage born in Derby, February 28.

1751 Marries Elizabeth Woolley of Mickleover.

1752 Son Charles baptized at St Alkmund's, Derby, February 8.

1753(?)Buys paper-mill at Elford, near Tamworth in Staffordshire; lives at the mill.

1755 Son Edward baptized at St Peter's, Elford, January 1.

1758 Son John baptized at St Peter's, Elford, October 28.

1770 Expansion of Elford mill.

1780 Failure of business venture with partners.

1782 *Mount Henneth* published anonymously (as were all the novels). Some of Bage's letters to Hutton from this year survive in the Birmingham Public Library, Local Studies Library.

1784 *Barham Downs.*

1788 *James Wallace.*

1791 Birmingham Riots, evidence of the increasing political animosity of the times.

1792 *Man as He Is.*

1793 Death of his youngest son; moves to Tamworth, but retains the mill.

1796 *Hermsprong, or Man as He Is Not.*

1801 Dies, September 1.

1810 Mrs. Barbauld includes *Hermsprong* in *The British Novelists,* with a Preface, Biographical and Critical.

1824 Scott includes *Mount Henneth, Barham Downs,* and *James Wallace* in Ballantyne's Novelist's Library, with a Memoir based on information from Catherine Hutton.

CHAPTER 1

Life and Times

I Early Life

R OBERT BAGE, one of the liveliest though least-known of late eighteenth-century English novelists, was born in the hamlet of Darley in the parish of St Alkmund's, Derby, in February 1728.[1] His father was a paper-maker, who taught the trade to his son; his mother died soon after he was born, and was succeeded by three stepmothers. A memoir by William Hutton records that when he first came to know Bage, then aged seven, he was already "the wonder of the neighbourhood" for his knowledge, which included Latin.[2] He was held up to Hutton, who was five years older, as a model for emulation. Scott, whose "Prefatory Memoir" of 1824, based on Catherine Hutton's recollections, is the fullest early account of Bage, believed him to have been brought up as a Quaker,[3] but there is no conclusive evidence of this.[4] Nevertheless, the strongly nonconformist element in Bage's later outlook may well be related to his background and upbringing, on which there is little information.

In 1751, at the age of twenty-three, Bage married Elizabeth Woolley of Mickleover.[5] Soon after this, he moved to the quiet Staffordshire village of Elford, between Lichfield and Tamworth on the River Tame, and acquired a paper-mill there.[6] In this area he spent the remaining fifty years of his tranquil life. Godwin saw the house at Elford where Bage lived for the first forty years. It was "floored, every room below-stairs, with brick, and like that of a common farmer in all respects. There was, however, the river at the bottom of the garden, skirted with a quickset hedge, and a broad green walk."[7] A sale-bill of 1804 described the property as "Consisting of a neat Dwelling House, with Out-Buildings; most desirably well constructed Mill for Corn and Paper; and upwards of Six

11

Acres of land."[8] Confirmation that Bage milled corn as well as paper is to be found in his having insured, in 1756, both mills under the same roof, which was not an unusual combination.

In 1756, too, Bage came to a business agreement with William Hutton, who had by then settled in Birmingham, "pleased with the active spirit of the people," and set up there as a bookseller.[9] Hutton later wrote about the agreement:

Robert Bage, an old and intimate friend, and a paper-maker, took me to his inn, where we spent the evening. He proposed that I should sell paper for him, which I might either buy on my own account, or sell on his by commission. As I could spare one or two hundred pounds, I chose to purchase; therefore appropriated a room for the reception of goods, and hung out a sign: THE PAPER WAREHOUSE. From this small hint I followed the stroke forty years, and acquired an ample fortune.[10]

Hutton was the better businessman, and had the self-confidence of his success. By his industry and efficiency he was to become one of the most prominent citizens of expanding Birmingham.

It was probably soon after this that Bage became acquainted with the writer and scientist Dr. Erasmus Darwin. Bage told Godwin in 1797 that he had known Darwin for forty years, and mentioned John Whitehurst, the geologist and experimental scientist later associated with the Lunar Society, as one of "the other acquaintances of his youth."[11] The word youth would leave one to suppose that Bage knew these men in Derby (where Whitehurst had a watchmaker's shop), but the period of years mentioned in connection with Darwin suggests that the acquaintance with him began at about the time of Darwin's move to Lichfield in 1756. In view of the proximity of Tamworth to Lichfield this is likely. Darwin was one of the most remarkable men of his time, and his wide range of interests and freedom from prejudice must have made him agreeable to Bage.[12]

These seem to have been years of tranquil married life, and during them three sons were born.[13] Bage taught himself music, and French and Italian, snatches of which languages he introduced, often inaccurately, into his novels. In 1760 he decided to study mathematics and went into Birmingham for weekly lessons with a well-known teacher, Thomas Hanson. Hutton sometimes attended, and he noticed how soon Bage was able "to teach his master, nay, even set him fast," though he attributed this in part to Bage's "easy fluency" contrasted with the mathematician's lack of verbal dexterity.[14] Bage later told Godwin that for twelve years he devoted the three hours an afternoon he allowed himself for study to mathematics, and that this "destroyed the eagerness of his attachment to poetry," which he had felt in his youth.[15] As yet, he made no attempt at writing.

Bage's business became even more closely associated with Hutton's in 1761, through an arrangement which meant that Hutton became Bage's sole customer. Hutton noted:

Entered into a verbal agreement with R. Bage to purchase all the goods he made — all treaties are excellent that suit both parties to keep.[16]

The bargain operated well for Hutton at least. He recorded later that he had paid Bage an annual average of £500 and that in forty-five years "he never gave me one cause of complaint."[17] Clearly Bage was an efficient miller who produced paper of good quality.

In 1766, presumably for financial reasons, Bage sold his mills to the Earl of Donegall for £2,000 but was granted the tenancy on a sixty-one-year lease for £46 p.a.[18] Donegall had bought Fisherwick Hall in Staffordshire in 1758, the year after inheriting his title at the age of eighteen. He married in 1761, and five years later engaged Capability Brown to remodel the Elizabethan manor-house and the grounds. The work proceeded from 1766 to 1774 and was on a lavish scale. A vast Palladian mansion was built, with a Corinthian portico; the drawing room was decorated by Joseph Bonomi, and the ceiling painted by M. Rigaud. A hundred thousand trees were planted.[19] In his landlord Bage had an outstanding example of the "conspicuous consumption" which such Augustan moralists as Smollett and Goldsmith vigorously deplored. In 1788 Donegall was ironically described in a letter as "a serious, well-disposed nobleman" who "had expended £20,000 on books not yet opened, and £10,000 on shells not yet unpacked."[20] Politically he was adept enough to achieve an English barony (Baron Fishwick, County Stafford, 1790) and an Irish marquisate (Earl of Belfast and Marquess of Donegall, 1791). Thus, although Horace Walpole thought him "a very weak creature,"[21] Donegall had some political talent. He may well have contributed to Bage's unfavorable view of the traditional ruling class. Certainly Bage must have known of the grounds of Fisherwick where, as the agricultural expert William Pitt noted in 1794, "the genius of a Brown" and the generosity of the owner had "conspired to render a dreary morass one of the most delightful spots in Nature."[22]

The quiet orderliness of Bage's life at Elford, together with his striking liveliness of mind, is well conveyed in the laudatory periods of Hutton's tribute to his friend in his *History of Derby,* published in 1791:

Although Fortune never made him conspicuous in the great world, she gave him what is preferable, affluence and content. In directing a paper-mill, may be found that head which is able to direct empires; that judgement, which can decide in difficult cases; a penetration, which can fathom the human heart, and comprehend various systems of knowledge; a genius, which constitutes the companion for Newton in Philosophy; for Handel in Music; for Euclid in Mathematics; a master of the living and dead languages; and all, like the wealth of a merchant who rises from nothing, acquired by himself.... That rectitude, which is rarely found, is here obscured from the public eye; but is a pearl of great price, and a credit to our species.[23]

For Hutton, a more ambitious man, Bage was a notable example of the contented mercantile spirit. The way in which Bage's "affluence" is said to serve his "content" suggests an affinity with the traditional ideals of simplicity and moderation embodied, for example, in Smollett's *Humphry Clinker* of 1771, and it was on such traditional bases that Bage's social thinking was built.

Scott quotes a letter, written in 1816 by Bage's eldest son, Charles, to Catherine Hutton, contrasting his father with hers:

Their success in life was very different; my father never had a strong passion for wealth, and he never rose into opulence. Your father's talents were continually excited by contact with "the busy haunts of men"; my father's were repressed by a long residence in an unfrequented place, in which he shunned the little society he might have had, because he could not relish the conversation of those whose minds were less cultivated than his own.[24]

Bage's appearance is described thus by Scott:

In his person, Robert Bage was rather under the middle size, and rather slender, but well proportioned. His complexion was fair and ruddy; his hair light and curling; his countenance intelligent, yet mild and placid. His manners were courteous and his mind was firm.[25]

As a father his behavior was enlightened:

> He behaved to his sons with the unremitting affection of a father; but, as they grew up, he treated them as men and equals, and allowed them that independence of mind and conduct which he claimed for himself.[26]

Although Elford was a quiet village, with a population of only 383 in 1801, the area was beginning to change. Thus Bage experienced locally something of the changes affecting the whole country. William Pitt summarized a local farmer's account of the effects of enclosure:

> The greater part of the parish of Elford was common field until 1765, when an Act was obtained for an inclosure. By inclosure rents have been trebled and the tenants are better able to discharge them. About five hundred acres out of nineteen hundred are in tillage, which we suppose brings as much grass to market as the whole parish did in its open state. The quantity of cheese now made in proportion to that made prior to the inclosure is more than three to one; the proportion of beef and mutton produced on the land is still greater, as much as ten to one, for though there were sometimes many sheep kept in the common fields, they were so subject to rot that little or no profit arose to the farmer, or produce to the community. Respecting population there were, prior to the inclosure, fifty-seven houses; there are now seventy-six, and 360 inhabitants; the increase is not due to manufactures, merely to improved cultivation, which demanded more labour.[27]

Pitt himself noticed the change, though he described it less fulsomely. To him it looked like "a county just emerging from a state of barbarism."[28] Laborers earned 1/-to 1/6d. a day plus beer in the early 1790s; beef and mutton were 3½d. to 4½d. a pound, butter 10d. to 1/-.

Much more striking than the agricultural changes were those arising from the development of industry in Staffordshire. In the north of the county the potteries were rapidly expanding, with Josiah Wedgwood's works at Etruria achieving a wide reputation. To the south, change was equally rapid. The first *History of Birmingham,* published in 1782, was written by William Hutton with mercantile enthusiasm. For him, Birmingham after the Restoration was truly a heroine:

> But now, her growth will be amazing; her expansion rapid, perhaps not

to be paralleled in history. We shall see her rise in all the beauty of youth, of grace, of elegance, and attract the notice of the commercial world. She will add to her iron ornaments, the lustre of every metal that the whole earth can produce, with all their illustrious race of compounds, heightened by fancy, and garnished with jewels.[29]

The population increased from 35,000 to 70,000 between 1760 and 1801.[30] Matthew Boulton, one of the most remarkable and resourceful of early industrialists, brought the new Soho Manufactory into operation in 1762, and — especially after James Watt moved there in 1774 — it became widely known.[31] Already by 1765 £4,000 had been spent on extensions to the factory, which employed 600 workers. Boulton, "the ingenious proprietor," also established "a seminary of artists, for drawing and modelling,"[32] to which the heroine of Bage's novel *Man as He Is* (1792) was to belong. The German observer F. A. Wendeborn, who lived in England for many years, wrote in 1784 in the section of his *View of England* entitled "On Manufactures":

> It is said of the English, that they are not endowed with great talents for invention; but, whoever has seen the manufactories at Birmingham, and in many other places, will be easily convinced, that such an assertion is to be made with caution; and that they, certainly, are the most ingenious to improve inventions already made, to render them more perfect.[33]

Nor was the progress confined to industry and commerce. As Asa Briggs has remarked, there was in the developing industrial towns "an early period of cultural initiative."[34] The Lunar Society of Birmingham is striking evidence of this. From about 1766 meetings had started taking place in the locality for the discussion of various scientific and technical topics. Members of the group were eventually to include the industrialists Matthew Boulton and Josiah Wedgwood, the scientists James Watt, James Keir, and Joseph Priestley, the writers R. L. Edgeworth and Thomas Day, the geologist John Whitehurst, the botanist Dr. Withering, as well as the all-round man of ideas Erasmus Darwin.[35] The society has received its due recognition in R. E. Schofield's thorough study *The Lunar Society of Birmingham*. His conclusion is that its members were making "a deliberate application to solve the problems of industrializing England," and that in the society may be seen "the seeds of nineteenth-century England."[36] This is a just appraisal of the technological aspect, though it fails to emphasize the qualities of the good employer also shown by Boulton and Wedgwood in relation to their workpeople — an example too seldom followed by Victorian employers. Perhaps the best tribute to the society is that recorded by Leonard Horner on a visit to Soho in 1809, where he noted that its influence survived, "to the second and third generations, in a spirit of scientific curiosity and free enquiry, which even yet makes some stand against the combined forces of Methodism, Toryism, and the love of gain."[37]

It was the intellectual reputation of the Birmingham area that explains the gratification of Joseph Priestley, who was already well established as the leading chemist and one of the foremost Dissenting thinkers of the time, at his move there in 1780. He later wrote:

I consider my settlement at Birmingham as the happiest event in my life, being highly favourable to every project I had in view, philosophical or theological. In the former respect I had the convenience of good workmen of every kind, and the society of persons eminent for their knowledge of chemistry, particularly Mr. Watt, Mr. Keir, and Dr. Withering.[38]

There is no evidence that Bage knew of the Lunar Society as such; its members certainly did not advertise its existence. Hutton, for instance, made no reference to it in 1782. On the other hand, the rioters in 1793 apparently included among their slogans, "No Philosophers — Church and King for ever,"[39] clearly a reference to the number of people in the area known to be interested in science. In *Man as He Is* Bage refers to Dr. Priestley, Mr. Keir, and Erasmus Darwin, and to Birmingham as "a place scarcely more distinguished for useful and ornamental manufacture, than for gentlemen who excel in natural philosophy, in mechanics and in chemistry."[40] Bage certainly knew of, and sympathized with, the interests of the group, whether or not he knew many of its members personally. He could have met Priestley at the Huttons'. As Mrs. C. H. Beale noted in her account of Catherine Hutton, when commenting on the destruction of the Huttons' town house in the High Street in 1791:

At this house Miss Hutton enjoyed the society of many literary friends, Dr. Priestley, Mr. Berrington, Mr. Hamper, Mr. Robert Bage and others.[41]

But evidence goes no further than the possibility.

Priestley regarded the congregation he was called to serve at the

New Meeting as "the most liberal, I believe, of any in England."[42]
In Birmingham at this time Unitarianism was thriving, many of the
leading citizens being Unitarians, but there were meeting places or
chapels also of Quakers, Jews, Presbyterians, Lady Huntingdon's
Connexion, Roman Catholics, and Swedenborgians, and there
were large numbers of Congregationalists, Baptists, and Methodists, while at the same time new Anglican churches were being
built.[43] This suggests the vitality of Birmingham, as do other facts.
In 1779 the Birmingham Library was formed, with an annual
subscription of 30/-; it was reorganized by Priestley in 1781. By
1795, the earliest year for which a catalogue is available, the library
included four of the five novels then published by Bage, as well as
such other radical works as Thomas Holcroft's *Anna St. Ives* and
Bernardin de St. Pierre's *Indian Cottage*.[44] In 1784 a separate
Science Library was established. Triennial music festivals were held
from 1779 onwards; the General Hospital was founded in the same
year. The overall impression is of rapid development, not restricted
to industry. Hutton saw this as natural:

Civility and humanity are ever the companions of trade; the man of
business is the man of liberal sentiment; a barbarous and a commercial
people is a contradiction; if he is not the philosopher of nature, he is the
friend of his country.[45]

Bage's novels embody a similar mercantile confidence.

There is little information about Bage's life in the 1770s. A document in the William Salt Library dated 1770 shows that Bage had,
without consulting his landlord, taken down "one dwelling house"
to build a drying house for the paper-mill, and had removed the
"stones and divers other engines and utensils" from the corn-mill
in order to convert it also.[46] Bage signed a bond for £500 to the Earl
of Donegall to complete the rebuilding within six months and later
to include the new mill as part of the earl's property. This suggests
that Bage was expanding his production of paper. Hutton and
Godwin both record that from about 1765 for some fifteen years
Bage was a partner with two or three others (one of whom, according to Godwin, was Erasmus Darwin)[47] in a "wholesale iron manufactory," which eventually failed, with a loss to Bage of the large
sum of £1,500.[48] Godwin also mentions that after this, Bage
"returned once more to his village and to his mill,"[49] though it
seems unlikely that he was ever very far away.

II *Political and Intellectual Background*

It has been noted that Bage would have been aware of the fundamental changes just beginning in England, both from his experience of Elford and, much more strikingly, from his knowledge of what was occurring at Soho and in Birmingham. As a businessman he was very much part of the modern world, although his chosen place of living set him rather in the traditional countryside. It is a balance which is characteristic of the man revealed in the novels.

By the time he began writing, in the 1780s, the economic changes were beginning to show significant social and political results. It was becoming more and more obvious that the semifeudal style of government which had survived in the form of the Whig oligarchy of the early eighteenth century was no longer a satisfactory form of social organization. Groups of various kinds began to emerge seeking to change the status quo, including the various philanthropic bodies, and individuals then began to seek radical changes in such spheres as the administration of justice, the prison system, and the slave trade, till then a generally accepted form of commercial activity. George III came to the throne in 1760, and it was during his reign that economic and social changes and the resultant political conflicts became most marked. The numerous organizations which came into existence to press for reforms of various kinds are evidence of the changing situation. From the County Associations of the 1770s and the Society for the Abolition of the Slave Trade in 1787, we move to more directly political groups such as the Society for Constitutional Information (1780), the Friends of the People (1792), the London Corresponding Society (1792), and the opposing conservative organization, The Association for Preserving Liberty and Property against Republicans and Levellers (1793).

S. MacCoby in *English Radicalism 1786-1832* has argued that "it was during the struggle against George III's increasing domination of politics and Parliament, between 1762 and 1782, that modern British Radicalism was born."[50] Certainly there is incontestable evidence that as the century advanced, the consensus which had marked its middle years was breaking down. The later decades were marked by fierce political arguments: over Wilkes and the Middlesex elections; over the American War of Independence; and finally and most sharply, over the French Revolution. Many of these controversies are reflected in Bage's novels, which thus furnish evidence of the increasingly political temper of the times. Opinion tended to become polarized, with the defenders of the *status quo* and the critics of society each vehement in the expression of their own opinions and in the denunciation of their opponents'. As E. P. Thompson puts it, the seventeenth-century debate between upholders of property rights and levellers was reopened with comparable acerbity:

For 100 years after 1688 this compromise — the oligarchy of landed and commercial property — remained unchallenged, although with a thickening web of corruption, purchase, and interest.... To read the controversies between reformers and authority, and between different reforming groups, in the 1790's is to see the Putney Debates come alive again. The "poorest he" in England, the man with a "birthright," becomes the *Rights of Man:* while the agitation of "unlimited" members was seen by Burke as the threat of the "swinish multitude."[51]

The most direct literary expressions of the conflict are the major works of political argument which mark the period: Burke's *Reflections on the Revolution in France* (1790), Paine's *Rights of Man* (1792), and Godwin's *Enquiry Concerning Political Justice* (1793). The two attitudes in conflict are clearly shown in Burke's contrast between the English and French approaches to morals and politics: "We are afraid to put men to live and trade each on his own private stock of reason: because we suspect that this stock in each man is small, and that the individuals would do better to avail themselves of the general bank and capital of nations, and of ages."[52] For Burke, and for the English whom he characterizes, the sources of true values are nature, experience, and tradition. Godwin, on the other hand, devotes an important section of his *Enquiry* to "the Right of Private Judgement": "If there be any truth more unquestionable than the rest, it is that every man is bound to the exertion of his faculties in the discovery of right, and to the carrying into effect all the right with which he is acquainted."[53] Godwin, and in this he is representative of the radical writers, trusts private judgment; indeed, he regards its exercise as a moral duty. Paine's attitude is similar. As A. O. Aldridge wrote in *Man of Reason:* "It is no accident that Paine should have written both the most influential book on deism and the most influential tracts in English on the revolutions in America and France. The same impulse which made him question the role of privilege in society made him doubt authority in religion."[54] This emphasis on private judgment is to be found also in Mary Wollstonecraft's *A Vindication of the Rights of Woman* (1792): "Men, in general, seem to employ their reason to justify prejudices, which they have imbibed, they can scarcely trace how, rather than to root them out. The mind must be strong that resolutely forms its own principles; for a kind of intellectual cowardice prevails which makes many men shrink from the task, or only do it by halves."[55] The reliance on the free exercise of human reason places these writers in the main intellectual tradition of the eighteenth century, that of the Enlightenment, whose central effort, as Copleston has put it, was to substitute " 'free thought,' the autonomy of reason, for authority."[56] Earlier English exponents of this tradition were such distinguished Dissenters as Richard Price and Joseph Priestley.[57] Price himself lived just long enough to see the French Revolution, and eloquently expressed the hopes which it aroused in him in the sermon which formed the starting point for Burke's onslaught: "And now, methinks, I see the ardor of liberty catching and spreading; a general amendment beginning in human affairs, the dominion of Kings changed for the dominion of laws, and the dominion of priests giving way to the dominion of conscience."[58]

Particular aspects of English society which came in for criticism from such writers as Paine and Godwin included the institution of aristocracy, together with its associated forms of behavior, especially dueling; colonialism, as it affected America and India; religious establishment; and, less emphatically in the male writers, the allocation to women of an inferior social role. The enthusiasm of the radicals was for the alternative ideals of greater social equality (including increased respect for women, and for such exploited groups as the Negro slaves and the harassed Indians) and religious toleration.[59] They regarded the development of commerce and the spread of education, especially of scientific knowledge, as conducive to social progress, and this they believed to be characteristic of the age they were living in — at least until the mid-1790s, when the Terror in France led to a conservative swing in public opinion in England. Gary Kelly, in his informative discussion of Bage, Godwin, Holcroft, and Mrs Inchbald, has recently characterized the Jacobin attitude very clearly: "What the English Jacobins and the English Jacobin novelists insisted on was simply that reason should decide the issue in human affairs and human government, not power based on money, age, rank, sex, or physical strength."[60] In making that claim Bage had to take up a critical attitude toward many prevailing British institutions, and he was therefore appropriately to take his place in the rogues' gallery of *The Anti-Jacobin Review,* in February 1800,[61] along with other prominent radical writers. All his novels reveal the cast of mind which inevitably led him to that position.

III   *Novel Writing*

Bage gave as the unusual reason for starting to write novels his need to distract himself from his financial loss, rather than the aim of publication. Indeed, according to Godwin, "He [Bage] believes he should not have written novels, but for want of books to assist him in any other literary undertaking."[62] At all events, he sold his first novel, *Mount Henneth,* to Thomas Lowndes for the good price of £30.[63] It was published anonymously in 1782,[64] and welcomed by the *Monthly Review* with warm praise:

. . . we do not remember that we have, for many years, had the satisfaction of reviewing a work of this kind, that abounds with more lively strokes of wit and sallies of fancy; with more judicious reflections, or pleasing and interesting characters.[65]

The period at which Bage began to publish was not distinguished for its literature. Leigh Hunt, looking back to that time in his *Autobiography* (1850), described the situation then:

In the world of literature and art, Goldsmith and Johnson had gone; Cowper was not much known; the most prominent poets were Hayley and Darwin; the most distinguished prosewriter, Gibbon. Sir Joshua Reynolds was in his decline, so was Horace Walpole. . . . Miss Burney, afterwards Madame D'Arblay, surprised the reading world with her entertaining, but somewhat vulgar novels; and Mrs. Inchbald, Mrs. Charlotte Smith, and a then anonymous author, Robert Bage (who wrote *Hermsprong,* and *Man as He Is*), delighted liberal politicians with theirs.[66]

This description telescopes the 1780s and 1790s, but the names of Hayley and Darwin as poets, and Fanny Burney as novelist, show the absence of greatness in both areas. Poetry was soon to be redeemed by the great Romantics, but the novel had to wait some twenty years for Jane Austen and Scott. In the meantime, as J. M. S. Tompkins put it in her fine study *The Popular Novel in England, 1770–1800,* "the chief facts about the novel" were "its popularity as a form of literature, and its inferiority as a form of art.''[67]

Against this background, Bage's novels stood out for their liveliness and intelligence. He went on to publish *Barham Downs* in 1784, *The Fair Syrian* in 1787, and *James Wallace* in 1788. Modest popularity is suggested by the fact that *Mount Henneth* and *The Fair Syrian* were pirated in Dublin in the years of their publication, and *Mount Henneth* also had a second London edition in 1788.[68] *The Fair Syrian* was well received by the *Monthly Review:*

...it is no little satisfaction to us, we say, to meet with a writer like the present, who to ease and correctness of expression unites that very essential requisite of a good novelist — a talent for nice and accurate delineation of character: who contrasts his several personages with considerable skill and ability: who gives to them their appropriate language, spirit, and manners; and who firmly presents us with a fable or story, tolerably harmonious in all its parts.[69]

The author — still anonymous — was praised as ''something more than a novel-writer ... a philosopher and friend of man.'' On the other hand *James Wallace* received mixed reviews: the *Monthly Review* felt that the author had not ''advanced his fame by the present publication'';[70] the *Critical Review* described the novel as ''the collected shreds of his other novels'' and felt that the author was exhausted;[71] but the *European Magazine* was enthusiastic:

This is a sensible and entertaining novel. The story, which in many parts is deeply affecting, is told in a series of letters; but the Author has judiciously avoided the dull tautology which in general accompanies epistolary correspondence. The characters are extremely well conceived, and not badly sustained. Two of them appear to possess the recommendation of novelty. We mean those of Paracelsus Holman and Paul Lamounde, the latter of which would make no contemptible figure upon the stage. The incidents are natural and interesting, and the manners a faithful transcript from life. It incites the mind to laudable pursuits by inculcating the useful belief, that virtue and abilities, however they may for a time lie obscured, will ultimately meet with their reward. A pure spirit of benevolence and philanthropy breathes through the whole of it, and we may safely pronounce it to be a work that will not only please the understanding but improve the heart.[72]

James Wallace was the first of Bage's novels to be published by William Lane at the Minerva Press, which was notable for its com-

mercial success rather than its literary standing — Lamb was later
to call "the common run of Lane's novels" the "scanty intellectual
viands of the whole female reading public."[73] The fact that Lane
published Bage's later novels suggests that, despite their satirical
commentary on the age, they were good commercial propositions.
It is also ironical in view of Lane's conservative political outlook:
he was evidently more concerned about the success than the sentiments of his publications.[74]

From 1782 onwards some of Bage's letters to Hutton survive; the
manuscripts are in the Birmingham Public Library. Although most
of them are concerned with matters of business, even these display
the "vivacity, witty turns, and fine humour, spontaneously spring-
ing, without effort, from the heart"[75] which Hutton ascribed to the
correspondence as a whole. It is regrettable therefore that only
some 150 letters survive out of the thousand which Hutton says he
received. Many of the letters were written to urge Hutton to pay his
bills, in a variety of good-tempered ways, and many also complain
of the excise duties on paper. On August 1, 1787, Bage wrote:

Oh how I wish thou wouldst bend all thy powers to write a history of
Excise — with cases — showing the injustice, the inequality of Clauses in
acts — and the infernal direction every new one makes toward the oppression of the Subject — *It might be the most useful book extant.*[76]

Bage's integrity is suggested by the ending of a letter of February
23, 1789:

It is a certainty of this makes me run rope paper too thin — Of this fault
however I must mend — and will mend — whether you can or cannot
mend my price. I had rather lose some profit than sink a tolerable name
into a bad one.[77]

A similar spirit of mercantile rectitude and self-respect pervades his
novels.

Bage never allowed himself, however, to become completely
immersed in business, and his continuing intellectual curiosity is
shown by his membership in the Derby Philosophical Society at this
time. Erasmus Darwin had moved from Lichfield to Derby in 1782,
and with characteristic energy had formed a society there, which
began to meet in 1783. Robert Bage of Elford, the owner of a
paper-mill, is recorded as having been a nonresident member in

1788–89. The society had a lending library, and the Catalogue and Charging Ledger records twenty-four books borrowed by Bage between June 1788 and January 1789.[78] These are mainly concerned with science and medicine, suggesting that Bage was a serious student of contemporary developments, and they also include Thomas Reid's *Essay on the Intellectual Powers of Man (1785)*. It was of middle-class enthusiasts for ideas, like Bage, that the philosophical societies which were so notable a feature of late eighteenth-century intellectual life were largely composed.[79]

In 1791 Hutton published his affectionate portrait of Bage as a Derbyshire Worthy,[80] but in the same year the tranquillity of Bage's life — and much more, that of Hutton — was suddenly shattered by the unexpected violence of the Birmingham Riots. In July 1791 there were still Radicals in Birmingham bold enough to hold a dinner, attended by some eighty people, to celebrate ''the ideas of 1789.'' Priestley himself did not attend, and advised against its being held, since he was well aware of the bitterness of local feeling, partly occasioned by his controversies with the Anglicans (especially the Reverend Spencer Madan), which had political as well as theological significance. Already, according to Schofield, slogans were being daubed:

Children in Birmingham were taught to write ''Madan for ever, damn Priestley, No Presbyterians, Damn the Presbyterians'' on walls and houses.[81]

Nevertheless, the dinner took place, presided over by the moderate Anglican Keir, but it resulted in a large-scale riot. The mob, whom the magistrates failed to bring under control, probably from weakness (there being no effective law-maintenance force), raged throughout the town, destroyed the Old and New Meeting Houses of the Unitarians and Priestley's home at Fair Hill with much valuable scientific apparatus and research material, and attacked some twenty other buildings, mostly the homes of well-known Radicals and Unitarians and those whose prominence made them envied. Hutton's house and library were damaged, and he fled from Birmingham with his family. The riot lasted for another two days before the militia arrived. The county eventually, and reluctantly, paid some £35,000 damages to the victims of the riots. Most of the victims soon became reestablished, but Priestley and William Russell went soon after to America.[82]

Hutton wrote a vigorous and indignant account of the riots for his autobiography soon after they had taken place. He tells how he fled from Birmingham on Saturday, July 16, with his wife, son, and daughter, and stopped at Sutton Coldfield. Even here, however, they were not safe and were driven on "when the mistress of the house was seized with the fashionable apprehensions of the day, and requested us to depart, lest her house should be burnt."[83] Eventually they stopped at the Castle Inn at Tamworth, where the scene was nearly repeated:

"Though I have entered your house," said I, "as a common guest, I am a desolate wanderer, without money to pay, or property to pledge." . . . Their countenance fell on hearing it. I farther told them I was known to Mr. Robert Bage, a gentleman in the neighbourhood, whom I would request to pay my bill. My credit rose in proportion to the value of the name mentioned. Myself, my wife, son, and daughter, passed the night at the Castle at Tamworth.[84]

It was against this background of unusual violence, in which the underlying tensions of English society became dangerously prominent, that Bage wrote a longer and more personal letter to Hutton, dated July 25, 1791:

In this country, it is better to be a churchman, with just as much common sense as heaven has been pleased to give on average to Esquimaux, than a dissenter with the understanding of a Priestley or a Locke. I hope Dear Will, experience will teach thee this great truth and convey thee to peace and orthodoxy, pudding and stupidity. Since the riots, in every company I have had the misfortune to go into, my ears have been insulted with the bigotry of 50 years back — with, damn the presbyterians — with church and king huzza — and with true passive obedience and nonresistance — and may my house be burnt too, if I am not become sick of my species, and as desirous of keeping out of its way, as was ever true hermit.

But, my dear Will, for this heavy loss, hast thou not an account to settle with the hundred? or the county? This has been my great comfort in thy afflictions. I hope thou wilt not take it away from me.

I have already asked for the Bill at Tamworth, but Rice being out, could not get it. Will discharge it the first time I go.

Not a word of Mrs. or Miss Hutton. I wish thou wert a true catholic; and the penance for thy Sins, to write me every post — till I was satisfied. I would then know precisely the state of all your bodies and all your minds.

I do not pray half so earnestly for the recovery of your chattels — as of your tranquillities.[85]

Bage's affection and good sense are pleasingly shown here. He wrote again to Hutton on August 11 saying that he had "paid at the Castle — a fortnight since — only I gave nothing to servants or Chaise drivers. If any thing of that sort remains to be done pray let me know."[86] Hutton had evidently recommenced business by then, but he remained justifiably resentful of his unexpected treatment by his fellow townsmen, for whom he had such a high regard. He had not been at the dinner and was politically moderate.

The county was slow to pay compensation. On April 14, 1792, Bage wrote again, recommending tranquillity:

I do not know, my friend, if it is possible either for Mrs. or Miss Hutton, to recover their health, or any of you that tranquillity of mind you have been so long deprived of, on the sudden. The Huttonian habit of body and soul is at present too irritable. I hope I shall soon see the family nature, of a much stronger consistence. In the meantime, have the goodness to consider, that by the yielding to the attacks of fools and knaves — which are in themselves — Nothing — you please them, and torment yourselves. Do not so, Dear Will, — for why should thy folly, be as great as their malignity?[87]

The disruption of Birmingham at the time is vividly conveyed in a letter written by Matthew Boulton in August 1791:

The Town of Birmgm is quite unharmonied party spirit and Rancour tear all good neighbourhood to pieces but I am happy in living alone in the Country and am almost silent upon these dissonant Subjects. By minding my own business I live peacably and securely amidst the Flames, Rapin, plunder, anarchy and confusion of these Unitarians, Trinitarians, predestinarians and tarians of all sorts.[88]

Bage did not emulate the politic Boulton in being "silent" on these "dissonant subjects," but dealt with them in his last two novels.

IV   Man as He Is *and* Hermsprong

Man as He Is appeared in 1792, as usual anonymously, but (as Bage wrote to Hutton in July) there was a strong "report" that he was the author of the book. In a typically ironic manner, Bage asked Hutton to let him know of any favorable comments:

Thou saydst something in thy last about authorship — which makes me

suspect thou hast heard a rumour of my publishing lately. I have taken
great pains, and sunk money to Lane in the price, not to be known any
more as a novel writer — The title of my last I concealed even from my
sons — And yet — the report goes strongly that Man as he is, is mine.

What character it will have, I know not; but if thou hearest anything
said of it in Birmgm — if good, let me know — if bad, keep it to thyself. I
can digest flattery but hate correction.[89]

The anonymity was not always pierced. William Cowper heard the
novel attributed to his friend William Hayley, and wrote (to Lady
Hesketh) denying the attribution:

...nor is Hayley the author of *Man as He Is,* at least I think he would
have told me if he had, from whom he says he can keep nothing, not even
murther should he commit it.[90]

Cowper also wrote to Hayley himself about the book:

There has been a book lately published, entitled, *Man as He Is.* I have
heard a high character of it, as admirably written, and am informed that
for that reason, and because it inculcates Whig principles, it is by many
imputed to you. I contradicted this report.[91]

Cowper evidently obtained the book for himself soon after, for he
wrote to Samuel Rose in December: "We find it excellent —
abounding with wit and just sentiment, and knowledge both of
books and men."[92]

Bage's desire for anonymity may well have been the result of his
concern about the worsening attitude of the time to Liberal ideas,
but in fact *Man as He Is* was well received by the reviewers. The
Monthly Review considered that the novel belonged to "this superior kind ... which incites and animates the mind," though
discerning no unity in it.[93] The reviewer was in fact the vigorous
radical Thomas Holcroft, who was just publishing his own polemical novel, *Anna St. Ives.* The *European Magazine* published a very
favorable account of the novel in 1795:

The materials and texture of this Novel are so superior to those of which
this species of writing is generally composed, that we lament extremely
having so long neglected to peruse it, and announce its merits to the public. The author, who possesses a sound, discriminating, and improved
mind, has drawn his Characters, not from the mere suggestions of fancy,

as is usual with writers of this class, but from a clear, judicious and distinct view of their archetypes, as they exist in nature. In conformity to the title of his work, he has represented *"Man as he is,"* and seems to have taken Fielding and Le Sage for his model; but he has contrived to render his scenes contributory to the purposes of virtue, morality, and happiness.[94]

The reviewer was particularly impressed by Bage's power of characterization, which he praised at some length; he does not seem to have noticed the political overtones. The *Analytical Review* was normally favorable to radical ideas; its approving review did not appear until 1796, when Bage was referred to as "one of the favoured few" who combined "richness of mind and acquired knowledge blended with ... felicity of association," although it, too, described the novel as "rather a bundle of finely imagined incidents than a regular plot."[95] The reviewer on this occasion was Mary Wollstonecraft, another leading Radical.

In February 1793 Britain went to war with France, in defense of the Netherlands. The early idealism of the French Revolution had been followed in 1792 by the Terror, and the outbreak of war had the effect of making English Radicalism more politically suspect. Moreover, the economic strains of the war resulted in a rising cost of living and higher duties on paper, affecting Bage as employer of labor and paper-maker. He became very conscious of the prevailing hostility to liberal ideas. In January 1793 he commented to Hutton on Priestley's most recent publication — Part 2 of the *Appeal to the Public on the Subject of the Riots in Birmingham:*[96]

I am pleased to see the good doctor in print, on any subject except theology — but at present — Nothing from him will be attended to. No man's ear is open to anything but Church & King — and Damn the French — and Damn the Presbyterians. I abstain from all society, because respect for my moral principles is scarce sufficient to preserve me from insult on account of my political.[97]

At about this time Bage had the additional personal grief of the loss of his youngest son, and Godwin was told that this led him to move the four miles from Elford to the larger town of Tamworth, where he rented a house and could expect to enjoy more society. But he retained the house at Elford as "his security against the caprice or despotism of a landlord, who might expel him from Tamworth."[98] This fear no doubt had a political basis.

The letters often refer to the difficulties of the paper business, the rising cost of rags, the demands of the men for higher wages, increasing government taxation, and Hutton's reluctance to pay more for paper. Despite the situation, Bage generally achieved a sprightly tone, but in September 1794 he wrote to Hutton a letter which appears hurried and worried:

> This very morning, my men with mighty clamour, demand an increase of wages. I am under the necessity of complying, for they are low, but thou, much more than I, have the advantage of it.[99]

Bage was evidently a good employer: his benevolence is stressed in an oddly reading sentence of Hutton's memoir:

> His humanity will appear from his treatment of his servants, and even his horses, who all loved him, and whom he kept in old age.[100]

By Christmas Bage seems to have recovered his poise, writing wryly about the situation:

> Eat my breakfast quietly, you monkey? So I do, when my house don't smoak, or my wife scold, or the newspapers tickle me into irritation, or my men clamour for another increase of wages — for I have granted one of about £20 per Annum. But I must get my bread by eating as little of it as possible, for my Lord Pitt will want all I can screw of Overplus — No matter. This only comes to wish thee a merry Xmas and the rest of the annual household stuff.[101]

But times were clearly difficult.

The situation had hardly improved by 1796, and in a letter of July Bage neatly related his business relationship with Hutton to larger political issues:

> To be sure, thou hast been my sovereign long; and I never wished thee other than a long and happy reign. But to reduce thy subjects to bread and water, is the way to make them hang themselves, or rebel.[102]

The postscript to a letter in September refers directly to the political situation, as well as economic difficulties:

> Another meeting amongst my Men — Another rising (the 3rd) of wages. What will it all end in? Wm Pitt seems playing off another of his *alarming* manoeuvres agst the meetg of parliament — Invasion — to scare us into a quiet parting with our money.[103]

Public affairs could not be kept out of business life.

Despite his problems Bage managed at this time to write his last and most successful novel, *Hermsprong, or Man as He Is Not,* published, again at the Minerva Press, in 1796. Critical comments were generally favorable. The *Analytical Review* approved of its having "a more complete plot" than its predecessor, and felt that Bage had skillfully modified "Voltaire's Huron" (the title under which *L'Ingénu* appeared in English)[104] The *British Critic,* although disapproving of some of the principles expressed in the novel, felt it to be "far superior to most publications of the kind," and also praised the author for obtruding his sentiments "with no intemperate warmth."[105] In the *Monthly Review* for September William Taylor wrote a full and, on the whole, favorable critique. He criticized the structure of the novel, but was impressed by the qualities represented in its rational hero, Hermsprong, whom he described as "a prominent and fine delineation of the accomplished, firm, frank and generous man, worthy to be impressed as a model for imitation."[106] Taylor also related the novel to others expressing the "new philosophy," notably "Voltaire's Huron" and "the systematic sincerity and philosophic courage of Frank Henley in Holcroft" — Henley being the hero of Holcroft's *Anna St. Ives* of 1792. The fact that the reviews tend to judge *Hermsprong* on more ideological grounds than its predecessors is partly due to the novel itself, and partly to the more combative political atmosphere that had built up during the French war. Nevertheless, these reviews show that free discussion of ideas was still possible in wartime England. The Dissenters continued to be influential in the press at the time. The *Monthly Review,* the *Critical Review,* and the *Analytical Review* were all published by the radical bookseller Phillips, and they were consistently attacked in the conservative *Anti-Jacobin.*[107]

Although *Hermsprong* was published anonymously, the anonymity cannot have been strictly maintained, for when in June 1797 the noted radical philosopher William Godwin set out with Basil Montagu on a summer tour passing through the Midlands, he coupled Bage with Darwin as a sympathetically minded local writer worth visiting. In the event, the travelers missed Darwin, from whom they had intended to obtain an introduction to Bage, but Godwin decided to go on and introduce himself. Mrs. Darwin told them that Bage was "the Doctor's very particular friend."[109] The letters of Godwin to his wife, Mary, recording this meeting provide

one of the liveliest pictures of Bage. The people at the mill, at
Elford, where Godwin called, said that Bage normally came there
from Tamworth three times a week, and told Godwin to look out
for "a short man, with white hair, snuff-coloured clothes, and a
walking-stick."[110] Godwin met Bage, who characteristically had a
book in his hand, and got out of his chaise to talk and walk with
him:

> This six or seven miles was very fortunate, and contributed greatly to
> our acquaintance. I found him uncommonly cheerful and placid, simple in
> his manners, and youthful in all his carriage.[111]

Bage told Godwin his life-story and spoke also of his philosophical
outlook:

> He has thought much and, like most of those persons who have con-
> quered many prejudices and read little metaphysics, is a materialist. His
> favourite book on this point is the *Système de la Nature.*[112]

The conversation was so enthralling that Godwin felt no incon-
venience in waiting for his first meal of the day, having started out
at six in the morning, until dinner time at two o'clock. The scene
puts both men in an attractive light. Godwin's final comment on
Bage is that of a Londoner:

> I should have added to the account of Mr. Bage, that he never was in
> London for more than a week at a time, and very seldom more than 50
> miles from home. A very memorable instance, in my opinion, of great
> intellectual refinement, attained in the bosom of rusticity.[113]

And Mary, though she reproached Godwin for his late return from
the tour, remarked, "I did not wonder, but approved of your visit
to Mr. Bage."[114] She had reviewed *Man as He Is* in the previous
year. Thus had Bage achieved the respect of leading representatives
of English radical thought.

Unfortunately no letter remains giving Bage's impressions of
Godwin. Most of the later letters refer to the difficulties of the
paper trade, but still maintain a lively tone, as in a reproach to
Hutton in February 1797:

> But I have received good at thy hands, and shall I not receive evil?
> Besides every thing in this the finest freest best of all possible countries,
> grows worse and worse, and why not thee?[115]

By this time Hutton had retired from control of his business, although he continued to help his son Thomas to run it. That Bage remained firm in his attitudes may be seen from a letter of October to William about the latter's walking tour to Hadrian's wall:

Thou hast returned from the sublime of nature to the dull consideration of selling dear and buying cheap — which — except killing men — is now the sole study of the good English people.[116]

And a postscript retained the same flavor:

Make my Comp[ts] to Mr. Thomas H and scold him for having a spirit of trade less oppressive than his father's.[117]

Nevertheless, Bage wrote to Hutton in March 1800 that "the chain that connects us cannot be snapt without giving me pain almost to torture."[118] He was evidently attached to Hutton despite the terms of their business relationship.

For the New Year of 1800 Bage had sent the Huttons a pleasant message in his characteristic free-spoken manner:

I desire that our friend Wm. will inform Miss Hutton, that I have thought of her some hundred times perhaps since I saw her — insomuch that I have feared I was falling in love — and if she takes the vows — as she did not assure me she would now — Que devinerai-je? I suppose my french is bad — but desire her to mend it. And accept with Mrs. Hutton my comp[ts] for the season, and my sincere desire that each may be as happy as a good husband and virginity can make them.[119]

In March Bage again attempted to get Hutton to increase his payments:

This day I am 70. . . . But I should not have thought necessary to announce this sublime intelligence to thee by letter, if a necessity of a different kind had not compelled me to write. . . . It is that of calling thy attention to a new code of prices for paper. . . . Rags are risen.[120]

The opening statement presents a problem for the biographer as it contradicts the normally accepted date for Bage's birth, given by Hutton, and attested by the St. Alkmund's register, of February 1728. The change of calendar to the New Style in the 1750s would account for the difference of days, but hardly for the disparity of years. The date of 1730 for Bage's birth fits in with the information from Godwin that Bage was sixty-seven when they met, although Godwin's belief that this was "exactly the same age as Dr. Darwin" must be set beside the fact that Darwin was born in 1731.[121] Perhaps Bage was less accurate in these matters than was the business-like Hutton. In August Bage visited Darwin, and again met Godwin.[122]

In January 1801 Bage wrote to Hutton more strongly than usual, though not without an attempt at humor:

> I looked for the anger thou talkedst of in thy last, but could not find it — And for what wouldst thou have been angry, if thou couldst? Turn thy wrath away from me, and direct it against the winds and the fogs — In future I fear it will be directed against the Collectors of dirty rags in London and Germany — where the prices have increased — are increasing — and ought to be diminished — But will not be so — because we begin this Century by not doing what we ought to do — What we shall do at the end of it, I neither know nor care.[123]

Amid these difficulties, Bage retained his sympathy for the poor. In March, after again teasing Hutton about his tight handling of business affairs, Bage referred compassionately to the unemployed Birmingham button-makers: "the poor devils should Eat — which how they can do without making buttons, I cannot think."[124] Hutton tells of a visit from Bage in Birmingham in the spring of 1801 when Bage's appearance already suggested his approaching death:

> When we parted, I took what I thought an everlasting farewell. As he went out of the house, he shook hands with my nephew (a boy of thirteen) and, with a smile, "Farewell my dear lad, we shall meet again in heaven!" Though spoken in the jocular style, it seemed to indicate a sensibility of his approaching end.[125]

Bage died on September 1, 1801, leaving a widow and two sons. In his autobiography for the year Hutton noted two major, if dis-similar, events. The first was his walk from Birmingham to view Hadrian's wall:

> The second occurrence was the loss of my worthy friend Robert Bage, whom I had known 66 years, and with whom I had lived upon the most intimate terms of friendship during 51; a person of the most extraordinary

parts, and who has not left behind him a man of more honour or generosity.[126]

Of the published obituaries of Bage, that in the *Derby Mercury* gives the impression of having been written from some personal or local knowledge:

On Tuesday (Sept. 1st 1801), at Tamworth, in the 72nd year of his age, after a long and painful illness, Mr. Robert Bage, of that place. The kind benevolent affections were closely interwoven with his nature, and his mind was of a firm and manly cast, and of the most scrupulous integrity. His gentle and unassuming manner formed a striking contrast to the vigour of his understanding. He was distinguished by great mental acquirements, and was the author of *Hermsprong* and other admired literary productions.[127]

From what we know of him, Bage seems to have deserved the tribute.

CHAPTER 2

Mount Henneth: *A Practical Utopia*

MOUNT HENNETH was published in 1782, and a pirated edition appeared in Dublin in the same year. A second edition was published in 1788, and Sir Walter Scott included it in his *Ballantyne's Novelist's Library* in 1824. In writing his first novel Bage found it convenient to take another novel as his starting point. In 1779 S. J. Pratt had published, under the pen-name of Courtney Melmoth, *Shenstone-Green: or, the New Paradise Lost. Being a History of Human Nature. Written by the Proprietor of the Green.*[1] On the title page was a quotation from the poet William Shenstone: "Had I a Fortune of Eight or Ten Thousand Pounds a year / I would build myself a Neighbourhood." In his *Essays on Men and Manners* Shenstone had followed this remark by the reflection, "perhaps a very natural and lively novel might be founded upon the inconvenient consequences of it, when put in execution."[2] Pratt followed up this suggestion. Early in the novel Matilda, daughter of Sir Benjamin Beauchamp, the narrator, reads to him the passage from Shenstone which "cost me forty thousand pounds." The novel records the frustrations of his attempt to establish a "neighbourhood" by the recalcitrance of human nature. The story is told in a lively and often amusing way, so that *Shenstone-Green* may be accounted a minor success in the manner of the novel of ideas, of which Swift's *Gulliver's Travels* and Johnson's *Rasselas* were the most distinguished earlier English examples.

In *Mount Henneth,* Mr. Foston undertakes a scheme similar to that of Beauchamp, but in a more practical spirit. As he writes to Henry Cheslyn:

When this affair is finished, I shall hope to see you at the castle of Henneth; where, though I do not intend to follow the example of Sir Benjamin

Beauchamp in the peopling his Shenston-Green, I do hope to form a neighbourhood of the worthy and the good.[3]

Foston is a wealthy merchant with a wide experience of life, who
has lived and married in India, and is careful to select suitable
people for his scheme. The plot of the novel is arranged around this
recruitment, though this does not become clear until well on in the
book. The action concerns the tribulations of various young
people: Ann and Thomas Sutton, orphans dependent on unsympathetic relatives; John and Henry Cheslyn, young men of substance
and integrity; Julia Foston and her vivacious friend Laura Stanley,
with her snobbish brother and sister; and Camitha Melton, daughter of an independently minded American, captured on her way to
Europe by the villainous Captain Suthall, who tries to force her
into prostitution. At the end of the novel, a quadruple marriage
takes place: John Cheslyn and Julia; Henry Cheslyn and Camitha;
Tom Sutton and Laura; and Dr. Gordon (a benevolent and satirical
Scot) and Ann. Mr. Foston, Mr. Melton, Mr. Sutton, and Mrs.
Tyrrel are meanwhile given "armchairs and flannels" to help them
to enjoy the joyful scene. Bage's happy ending provides an effective reply to the moderate pessimism of Pratt's novel, with its concluding sighs of regret, "Alas, poor Shenstone-Green! Alas, poor
Human Nature!"

Bage does not, however, counter with a naive optimism. *Mount
Henneth* does not imply that all men are naturally good; it simply
counsels care and forethought in the selection of the participants.
Bage is a Utopian with his feet on the ground. His values, indeed,
are those of the Enlightenment, which more often found literary
expression in France than in England. Most of the characteristics of
the Enlightenment, as described for example by M. Hazard in
European Thought in the Eighteenth Century, can be found in the
novels of Bage. Hazard concludes his chapter on "Morals" in
"The City of Men" by noting the three "new virtues" typical of
the "new morality": these are Tolerance, Beneficence, and
Humanity.[4] These are also the attitudes of Mr. Foston, and they
underlie the whole novel.

I   Social Criticism

Bage's criticism of contemporary society finds expression in two
main ways: in the direct portrayal of social evils, and in the alterna-

tive kind of community established at Henneth Castle by the end of
the novel. The direct criticisms cover a variety of themes — snobbery, intolerance, extravagance, colonialism, dilettantism — but
the final effect, as embodied in the Castle community, is coherent.
The various criticisms emerge as parts of an overall radical view of
society, in deliberate opposition to traditional attitudes in many
spheres.

Mr. Foston, the self-made merchant, is central to the novel, and
his middle-class values are shown to be superior to those of the aristocracy, represented in the unattractive forms of the Stanleys and
the Caradocs. Sir Richard Stanley is sympathetic though weak, but
his wife, his son William, and his elder daughter Harriet are all
intensely snobbish. They try by every means to prevent the younger
daughter, Laura, from marrying the "tradesman" Tom Sutton.
Tom records a family conversation at which he has been present,
when Laura had challenged and aroused her sister's snobbery:

Insolent plebeian! says she [Laura] one day, when I had been endea-
vouring to persuade her I wanted only wealth to make just the sort of
gentle husband she ought to chuse; thou wantest wisdom also. Know, that
we people of a certain rank ought to keep ourselves to ourselves, and not
puddle ourselves with the clay and dirt of manufactures, or descend
towards the lesser gentilities. This was one of the wise precepts of our
grandmother, Harriet, was it not?

It was, sister, replies Miss Harriet, with a fine quality toss; and, notwithstanding your scorn, a precept that the good of society requires to be duly
observed.

The vigorous expression "puddle ourselves with the clay and dirt"
conveys the indignant repudiation of social superiority and
arrogance.

William Stanley pays court to Julia Foston, and becomes jealous
of John Cheslyn, whom he challenges to a duel. Cheslyn replies in a
dignified way which shows the absurdity of the convention of the
duel — a part of the aristocratic code which had been criticized by
novelists from the time of Richardson:

But I will have the satisfaction of a gentleman tomorrow morning; so
chuse your weapons.

The weapons of a gentleman, Stanley, are good sense and politeness;
never will I use any other against you if I can help it.

The neat reply gives a moral victory to Cheslyn and the post-chivalric ideal. William, described as "a gentleman of infinite heraldry," is clearly an unsuitable match for Julia Foston. He later transfers his affections to the daughter of Sir Owen Caradoc.

Intolerance is another aspect of the traditional outlook which Bage criticizes, mainly through the autobiography of Mr. Foston himself. He recounts how, as a young man, he had been dogmatic and fanatical in his religious views. On his way to take service with the East India Company, he quarreled with a young traveler, called Lewis; the captain of the ship punished them for brawling and gave some good advice:

> ...you have indirectly supposed, that the faculty of perceiving truth is yours exclusively, and that other people have not an equal right with yourself to the free communication of their own ideas ... reflect, that nothing in itself indisputable, can long be disputed, and that in propositions not absolutely demonstrable, the degrees of probability on which they rest are best known by free and ample discussion; the more truth they contain, the more visible it will become by examination.

Free enquiry is an ideal to supersede unthinking dogmatism. Foston, however, immediately becomes involved with Mrs. Sewel, who is a follower of the preacher Whitefield. She convinces him of the superiority of faith over works:

> I soon saw in the clearest light, the folly of trusting in those filthy rags of righteousness, which vain worldings call good works, and was almost convinced that the gallows was the best possible road to heaven.

But their "spirituals" come to a comic end when a lurch of the ship throws the young man upon the older woman, who defends her supposedly assaulted virtue with "prodigious agility." In a farcical scene she is "rescued" by one of the crew:

> This gentle squall brought in a sailor, who hallowed out, avast, d——m me! what boarding my boy without hailing the vessel! Come, damme, heave up.

The vigor of the eighteenth-century picaresque novel is felt here, but, unlike Smollett, Bage uses the farcical incident to lead to a moral formulation. When the sensible captain is told of this grotesque scene, he exonerates Foston from blame but suggests that in future he should try to become "a Christian and a Gentleman" rather than "a Monk or a Moravian": "Reflect, says he, how very different is the cant of a sect from the liberal language of a Christian at large." Bage, like Fielding and Smollett, is hostile to the Methodists for their supposed indifference to good works.[5] His emphasis is on social responsibility.

Foston is still not taught the value of toleration, however. In India, his religious zeal causes him to spit in the face of an idol in a "pagoda" of the "Gentoos," as a result of which he is thrown into the river. He is rescued, and given hospitality, ironically, by the priest of the temple himself. In a theological argument, Foston is unable to convince the priest that there is an "intrinsic excellence" in Christianity; the priest acknowledges One Great First Cause and urges the practice of toleration: "My son, be in charity with all religions; everything that is valuable in any, is truly the foundation of all." The device of confronting the orthodox Christian by a virtuous non-Christian is not unusual among eighteenth-century opponents of religious dogmatism.[6] It forms part of the strategy of Voltaire's *L'Ingénu,* for instance, a work which is usually said to have influenced Bage's last novel, *Hermsprong,* but whose effect on Bage is perhaps more pervasive. Foston's moral education is completed by his meeting an old Persian merchant, Duverda, whose daughter Caralia he eventually marries. Duverda belongs to no religious community and defines religion in the broadest possible terms as

...the silent meditation of a contrite heart, lifting up its humble aspirations to the author and preserver of all being, by what name soever called throughout the universe.

Duverda's outlook is like that described by Hazard in his account of "Natural Religion," when he summarizes prevailing views:

There is but one way to worship God, and that is to worship him inwardly, with heart and mind and soul. To acknowledge in a general sort of way a primary and Supreme Being; to lift up our hearts to him from time to time; to abstain from whatever is deemed dishonourable in the land in which we dwell; to fulfil certain prescribed social duties — these are the essential things: anything else is merely supererogatory.[7]

It is from this standpoint that Foston comes to see the wrongfulness of his earlier polemical religious attitude. He lives with Caralia and

Duverda for ten years, learning humility and charity — "how unjust it was to attach the idea of turpitude to speculative notions." Through these experiences Foston has become the active man of benevolence, unconcerned with abstractions, aiming to promote the happiness of his daughter and his fellow men by the exercise of the liberal virtues.

A further aspect of intolerance which is criticized concerns sexual morality, especially society's punitive attitude toward the "fallen woman." Mr. Foston arrives at Duverda's wrecked house too late to save Caralia from being raped by soldiers. When he wishes to court her, she holds back from him, saying that she has read in novels that the loss of a woman's "honour" is irretrievable. Foston dismisses this belief, addressing himself to Duverda: "It is to be found in books, Sir; and I hope, for the honour of the human intellect, little of it will be found anywhere else." But Bage's "laxness" on this point was to rouse Scott's indignation as late as 1824.[8] Bage is expressing the emerging feminist standpoint, which was to find its fullest embodiment in Mary Wollstonecraft. A similar emphasis is reflected in a letter from Ann Sutton deploring the commonly accepted idea of the double standard:

But in this good town, noone now, I perceive, affixes the idea of criminality to male incontinence. All the guilt, and all the burthen of repentance, fall upon the poor women. Such are the determinations of men.

There can be no doubt of Bage's radical sympathies on this important moral question.

An associated form of intolerance may be discerned in colonialism, to which there are a number of hostile references in the novel. As R. B. Heilman has shown, America and India were popular subjects for contemporary novelists; from 1771 to 1800 at least 50 percent of published novels included some reference to America, and something like 40 percent referred to India.[9] However, *Mount Henneth* was the second novel (after *Emma Corbett, or the Miseries of Civil War* by "Courtney Melmoth" in 1780) to give American affairs such prominence. The action of the novel takes place from August 1778. Henry Cheslyn has been a partner in a large American house, ruined by the "fatal year" of "the breach with the colonies." His brother John has to rescue him from bankruptcy. Camitha Melton and her father are presented in a heroic light in the story as victims of persecution and injustice who remain firm and courageous. They are captured by an English privateer on their way to France. Later, Camitha defends her virtue successfully against Captain Suthall with a pair of scissors, and her vigor is associated with her nationality: "She asserted her claim to independency and freedom (for she is an American) with great spirit and force of language...." Mr. Melton is imprisoned as an American spy, and refuses to seek release by becoming a "true British subject." John Cheslyn is impressed by his heroism.

Earlier in the novel occurs "The Soldier's Story," an interpolated narrative concerning a veteran of nine years' service in America, now lacking a left leg and a right arm, who is arrested for eating turnips from a farmer's field while starving. The discharged soldier was a stock character in the literature of the time, and often served as a focus for "sensibility." In Henry Mackenzie's *Man of Feeling* (1771), for example, the unfortunate and virtuous Edward, who compassionately allows an Indian prisoner to escape and is severely punished, arouses the reader's pity:

I was tried by a court-martial for negligence of my post, and ordered, in compassion of my age, and having got this wound in my arm, and that in my leg, in the service, only to suffer 300 lashes, and be turned out of the regiment; but my sentence was mitigated as to the lashes, and I had only 200. When I had suffered these, I was turned out of the camp, and had betwixt three and four hundred miles to travel before I could reach a seaport, without guide to conduct me, or money to buy me provisions by the way. I set out however, resolved to walk as far as I could, and then to lay myself down and die.[10]

Bage, however, adopts a tone closer to that of Pratt, whose Hackney Oldblade in *Shenstone-Green,* "being a man of no interest, hopped and begged on his majesty's highway." As Heilman noted,[11] there is no sentimentality in Bage's narrative, rather a vigorous irony:

In one of these [skirmishes], where we had come to close quarters, I had the luck to be well pinked and slashed; and having retreated as long as I could run, at length I laid down to die quietly like a hero.... I was got back to camp, where the surgeon dressed my wounds, and the next morning, to save time, sawed off my arm, and seared the stump. This was the most lively sensation I had ever experienced, but then it was glorious, and soldiers should be content.

Later, having been captured by the Americans, he is given the opportunity of working on a tobacco plantation:

My employment was to whip the negroes, which it was possible to perform with one arm, but, after a month's trial, mine was found too weak for the purpose, and I was discharged.

The humanitarian feelings of Mackenzie and Bage express themselves in strikingly different ways. In Bage's ironical tone, as in the interpolated narratives themselves, may be discerned the antisentimental influence of Fielding. The old soldier is finally given "comfortable settlement for life" at Henneth Castle.

The most direct expression of opinion about the American war occurs near the end of the novel and is made, not very plausibly, by a Hessian officer, a former mercenary in the British army in America:

To be serious, says he, although I have been engaged in it, and am, besides, the subject of a despotic prince, I like neither the principle, nor the general conduct: above all, I detest the sordid part we have taken in it — for daily bread.

Through this character, and through the suggestion of the benefits to be obtained by the reopening of trade between England and America, Bage makes his final criticism of the war. The *Monthly Review* was clearly in sympathy when it remarked on "the Author's sprightly manner of reasoning on a subject which grave politicians have not discussed with more solid argument, in long orations in the house, or in laboured productions from the press."[12] The American War had initially caused a surge of patriotic feeling in Britain, but it was consistently opposed by such liberals as Richard Price and Joseph Priestley on humane and ideological grounds,[13] and by many merchants and manufacturers on economic grounds.[14] As the expense and futility of the war became more obvious, opposition grew stronger, although peace did not come until 1783. Bage's attitude to the war is determined by both humane and economic views.

The East Indies also play a part in the novel. The young Thomas Sutton, when he has quarreled with his irascible uncle, decides to go there to seek his fortune, and his friends the Cheslyns offer him money to buy a lieutenancy in the company. Instead, however, he is invited by Mr. Foston to join the community at Henneth Castle, as

the agent or steward of the estate at £200 a year. Tom is relieved at
the change, and speaks of making better use of "the money once
destined to carry me where avarice and ambition is hourly employed in digging European graves." This remark succinctly conveys indignation at the exploitation of India. Mr. Foston's story,
told immediately after this by Tom, although it is largely a series of
picaresque adventures, has a similar moral. When Foston arrives at
Madras as a young adventurer, the political situation is described
with scorn:

The French and English, who never miss an opportunity of acquiring
power and plunder in the East, were assisting their [the Nabobs']　feeble
efforts to cut each other's throats.

Foston's idyllic marriage to the Persian girl Caralia — like
Melton's in America to "a Squaw" — supports the anti-imperialist
implications of Bage's comments.

　　A more traditional line of social criticism is followed by Bage
in his treatment of fashion and social ambition. Despite his belief
in commercial activity, Bage is as strongly opposed as an Augustan
moralist such as Smollett or Hogarth to the extravagance and
frivolity begotten by fashion upon social ambition. This is the
theme of several interpolated narratives; the ruin of Mr. Foston's
father on his promotion from curate to vicar; the decline of Hugh
Griffiths, shoemaker of Llan Llwyth, bankrupted by his wife's
extravagances; and the misfortunes of Sir Howell Henneth, who
dissipated a large fortune in his youth and ended his days in eccentric isolation, communicating with his servants through a
"tube" and living poorly in three rooms. Explicit comment on the
evil influence of fashion is made by Dr. Gordon, the sensible and
ironic Scot who serves as one of Bage's mouthpieces:

...as to govern one's self is found to be the most difficult of possible
things, the lady fashion steps in to free us from this intolerable thraldom.

Similarly, fashionable amusements are dismissed as both extrava-
gant and empty. Julia spends some time in London, but she avoids
Ranelagh, Vauxhall, the Tabernacle, and the "speaking ladies."[15]
She prefers the pleasures of domesticity:

From the bottom of my heart, do I pity all fine ladies and all fine gentle-

men, who are forced abroad for pleasure. The principal objection I have
to the manners of the age is, that that they are not social.

Through Julia, Bage is offering a concept of society different from
that of the aristocracy and those who ape their manners and ideals:
the focus is to be the home, not the public occasion.

Associated with this hostility to frivolous amusements is Bage's
condemnation of dilettantism. This is conveyed in the lively and
amusing treatment of two minor characters, the younger Caradocs.
They are described in a letter by Henry Cheslyn:

You would be astonished if I should give you the whole length and breadth
of their terrible accomplishments. The son is an eminent member of the
Antiquarian Society, the lovely daughter is monstrously enamoured of virtue; she minces snails to multiply the breed, kills cats in an air-pump, and
generates eels in vinegar.

Yesterday nearly our whole society were enjoying the cool air of the evening on the terrace. In the beautiful hanging pastures beneath, amongst
other quadrupeds, was your little roan mare, employed, as females sometimes are, in attending to the love of an ass. This animal was in love *à la
folie:* had broken through three barriers and was eager to reap the fruits of
this bold enterprise. To the philosophic eye all things are equal.

Miss Caradoc was the first struck with the view, and drawing Julia and
Laura to the wall, See! says she. Julia, blushing rosy red, withdrew her
arm and walked gently on. Laura, in a few seconds, followed and, burst-
ing into a laugh, See! cries she. Fie, Laura, says Miss Foston, walking on.
Brother, says the contemplative Miss Caradoc, you have constantly
asserted that copulation betwixt animals of different species, is unnatural
and always committed by a rape of the female — see the contrary. Miss
Melton and Mrs. Tyrrel turned across the area. Harriet followed something unwillingly.

Sister, says this solemn blockhead, the naturalists have not considered
an ass and a mare so much of a different species, as differing in specie. If
you can comprehend this distinction, you will observe that my observation
is not in the least invalidated by what you now see.

A learned dispute followed betwixt these two originals, in which the
whole science of generation was discussed. The brother maintained the egg
system; the sister, Lowenhoeek's. They ended at last with an enquiry into
the political cause of circumcision.[16]

The pedantic solemnity of the young Caradocs is well brought out,
first in the vigorous introductory remarks, mainly about Miss
Caradoc, then in the ludicrous scene on the terrace. The reactions
of the other characters are convincing: the sensitive Julia is embar-

rassed, the lively Laura amused. But the Caradocs themselves are
oblivious, safe in their own sense of intellectual superiority. The
scene is amusing in itself, and also places its participants on Bage's
moral scale; they are dilettanti. This is clear, too, from the account
of a visit to Miss Caradoc's "hall of philosophy" in which entertainment is offered rather than scientific activity:

Here you are entertained with puppets dancing in water, electric shocks,
and the humours of a magic lantern; phosphoric letters shine upon the
darkened wall, and living vipers crawl upon the ceiling; all the philosophic
sorcery was performed which Ozanam taught, and Hooper compiled. I am
enchanted, says Laura, it is so pretty an amusement for ladies.

The son of Sir Owen took his turn to reign. His domain is called the hall
of Archaeology. Here alone you will find something solid and sensible.
The young gentleman has ransacked Wales for Roman antiquities; and has
made a good collection of medals, of which he makes a proper historic
use. But, lest from these and other circumstances, which smell of common
sense, you might suspect him of degeneracy, he proves himself the son of
his father by about twenty tons of urns and vases: fragments of pavement,
Pateras, Capedos; Simpula and Lutini.

Again, the superficiality of the Caradocs is amusingly rendered in
the daughter's preference for spectacular scientific effects and the
son's for quantity rather than quality of archaeological material.

II   *The Henneth Castle Community*

The justification for claiming that the various elements of social
criticism and satire so far discussed amount to a coherent radical
view of society is to be found in the account given of the Henneth
Castle community with which the book ends. For this community
represents the opposite of the sophisticated manners of the time.
The spirit of the enterprise, at once idealistic, ironical, and sensible,
is suggested by the "document" drawn up by Dr. Gordon about the
arrangement:

A certain James Foston, Esq., having taken these premises into consideration, and considering it to be for the good of the species, if it could be
taught to *associate,* rather than to *herd,* doth appoint himself to be the
world's schoolmaster, and professeth to teach by example.

To carry this great work into execution, he hath established his dwelling
upon Mount Henneth, in the land of the ancient Britons. . . .

On the east side of the said mountain he hath determined, after the example of Sir Benjamin Beauchamp, to build himself a green, to be called the Green of association. But he hath not, like Sir Benjamin, determined to people the said green with vice and folly, to the utter exclusion of common sense and common gratitude; on the contrary, he chuseth to dwell therein. . . .

Any man of wealth, who will spend a moiety of his revenue in the purchase of felicity for others.

Any man of learning, who will take the trouble to compare the utility of Greek and Latin, with plough driving, and assign the preference without partiality. . . .

Any lady of quality, who loves her husband better than a rout, and her children better than flattery and admiration; Any lady who, having by accident slided in her youth, hath recovered the lapse by a chastity of ten unspotted years, and a prudence that hath sustained all the attacks of calumny, save only those of beaux and ancient maiden ladies at the tea-table. . . .

The virtues of unselfishness, social concern, domesticity, and tolerance are the antitheses of the fashionable selfishness, triviality, and censoriousness exhibited elsewhere in the novel. In choosing a Scotsman to make the values explicit Bage is drawing on the stock type of national character. J. O. Bartley has shown that the stage Scotsman of this period was generally shown as determined, independent, blunt, and well educated,[17] although English authors were often satirical in their treatment, whereas Bage is sympathetic. It is particularly Gordon's freedom from *idées reçues* which makes him a mouthpiece for Bage. His ironical tone about an enterprise in which he believes is like that of Bage's amusing Preface to the novel:

It is very easy to say, I wrote it for my own amusement, and published it to satisfy the importunity of some very judicious friends, who could not bear that so many beauties should lie concealed in the drawer of a cabinet. But as I intend to be upon honour with my reader, in point of veracity, I must candidly confess I have been determined by far different motives. In short my three daughters assure me, that I write in a very tasty manner; and that it is now two years, bating two months, since I made each of them a present of a new silk gown.

The relaxed tone, the avoidance of pretentiousness, the self-deprecation, are characteristic of the best parts of the novel.

These parts are seldom concerned with the depiction of character or the advancement of the plot: they generally deal with ideas and

attitudes. For instance, the description of Henneth Castle given by
Tom Sutton to his sister Ann shows Bage's awareness of the picturesque. The surroundings are described as "horribly delightful."
From the castle to the sea is a "waving walk ... bordered on each
side by shrubs and flowers," with branches leading in some direc-
tions to "close and retired walks," in some to "open glades," in
some to "wilds or wildernesses," in some to

deep shady groves, decorated with hermits' cells; others lead to grots,
ruins, alcoves, obelisks, or temples; two to beautiful springs of water,
received into capacious stone basons; one formed into an open bath for
gentlemen; the other into a covered one for ladies; both surrounded by a
grove of the most towering shrubs.

At the end of this catalogue of the picturesque, the reality is suddenly revealed:

In sober truth, this said western side of the hill is, at present, nothing more
or less than a pasture for goats; and what I have now said concerning it, is
a rude sketch of what it is to be, under the forming hand of Miss Foston,
whose taste is elegance itself.

In this way Bage is able to treat the cult of the picturesque, which
was then transforming the English countryside, in an ironical but
indulgent way.[18] The enthusiasm of Tom is reserved for an artificial
"cataract" to the North, two miles long, which combines utility
with its picturesqueness:

...it runs in a breadth of twelve feet only over rough stones laid for the
purpose, or roots and branches of trees; as much as is wanted for household purposes is brought into cisterns; the rest deflects to the eastern side,
and turning the water wheel of a corn-mill, runs thence into the valley,
where it is used for numberless rural purposes.

This emphasis on the practical is characteristic of Bage, as is also
the effective treatment of ideas.
    In the similar vein is Tom Sutton's description of the ladies at
Henneth Castle in terms of Alexander Cozens' *Principles of Beauty
Relative to the Human Head* (1778).[19] This book had engravings,
by Bartolozzi, of a series of heads without hair, while various hair
arrangements were enclosed, engraved on loose sheets of paper on
exactly the same scale as the heads. These could then be placed at

will on any of the profiles so that the reader could see for himself
the effect on the same face of different arrangements of the hair.
Cozens suggests that there is an ideal of pure beauty which is sep-
arable from character. In a letter describing the ladies at Henneth
Castle, Tom gives an amusing account of how their differing characters cause them to depart from the pure beauty of the ideal.

But the most important ideas for Bage are those embodied in the
Mount Henneth community at the end of the novel. These are not
presented ironically, although the idyll is given unusually practical
elements. There is a good deal of emphasis on work:

> . . . I propose, continues Mr. Foston, that every man amongst us should be
> a man of business, of science, and of pleasure. We must have manufac-
> tures, that other folk may be as happy as ourselves and that Julia's chil-
> dren may be brought up in the way they should go. We must have com-
> merce, or the manufactures will be useless.

Mr. Foston and Tom are to take charge of the lands and houses;
Mr. Melton and Henry are to deal with trade. Mr. Melton has had
experience of ship-building in Rhode Island and finds a suitable site
for his activity:

> Your timber will find the most profitable market; and, in two years, the
> business, in all its branches, may give employment to about one hundred
> of your people.

Dr. Gordon is to provide medical care, and has other projects of his
own:

> I understand something of my own country linen manufactory; Welch
> women may be taught to spin, and Welch land to bear flax. But, above all,
> I consult my own propensities in the erection of a dome to make glass
> bottles. I have marked a hill abounding with excellent flints for the pur-
> pose; and when we have made glass, man, it will be the easiest thing in the
> world to make spectacles.

Their spare time is to be divided between science and pleasure. Mr.
Foston describes the prospects:

> With regard to science, the whole range of natural philosophy lies
> before us. May it find successful cultivators. Let us pursue it, not as Dilet-
> tanti, but as men in earnest, to extend its boundaries. Let us divide the

country into regions, and each preside over his own.

As to the article called pleasure —

Leave it, says Laura, to your wives.

To this we gave an assent universal, on condition there shall be no monopolies.

The last letter, from Ann Gordon, tells of the happiness of Henneth Castle for the four months since the weddings, when Mr. Foston's plan is being carried out to the common delight of all. A true community has been created.

In this community at Henneth Castle Bage has created a bourgeois or mercantile version of the conventionally rural myth of idyllic felicity. The vision rendered with gentle nostalgia in Goldsmith's *Deserted Village* and with greater force and directness in Smollett's Greavesbury Hall in *Sir Launcelot Greaves* of 1760–62 (where "one would have thought that the golden age was revived in Yorkshire") is brought by Bage into contact with trade, science, ship-building, and glass-making. This lends an unusual air of definiteness and practicality to what is still an idyll. It also makes explicit the scheme of values lying behind the novel, which includes hostility to feudalism, distrust of religious dogmatism, and belief in the virtues of self-reliance, toleration, and good sense. Bage's ironical tone does not make him sound a revolutionary moralist, but the radical implications of his social philosophy are undeniable. *Mount Henneth* may be seen as the expression of that provincial radicalism, closely associated with the industrial development of the Midlands, which the Lunar Society also embodied.

III   *Technique and Influences*

The form which Bage adopted in *Mount Henneth,* that of the epistolary novel, was not particularly suited to the expression of ideas. No doubt he felt that the chance which the form gave for variety of character and action would be an advantage. With one pair of correspondents, Julia Foston and Laura Stanley, he succeeded in creating a lively contrast of characters. Such contrasts were frequent, in the wake of Richardson's Clarissa Harlowe and Anna Howe, but Bage exploits the device effectively. Julia is fond of serious reading, while Laura is a "mad-cap." She expatiates on the mutual advantage of their difference of character:

But you are a philosopher, and I am a mad-cap; *tant mieux,* we shall accommodate one another. You shall show me the cotyledons of flowers, and I will show you my last new cap. You shall entertain me with the generation of insects, and I will display my love-letters in amplest beau-spelling before you.

She is reproved by Julia for her flippancy:

My facetious friend can, if she pleases, give delight by her conversation, or her pen, without the aid of arch libertinism, the sly allusion, or the *double entendre.*

But Laura is unrepentant:

...I make my bends to your Cambrian highness, and humbly sue for the post of first maid of honour, if I am not unfortunately disqualified by wrong *conceptions.* I expect your highness's chastisement for this.

She is even able to retain her lightness of manner when writing to Julia about a friend at the convent, who had been sent there as a consequence of being found making love with a childhood boyfriend:

...and one day, when we thought she was busy at her prayers, she bolted into the room, and — catched us, —
    Doing what, Miss Thompson?
    Lord, Laura! How can you teize one so? I won't tell you a word more.

Laura ends the letter with a sardonic reflection: "I doubt not she will become as respectable a woman as a thousand others, whose fifteens — were very — ticklish." Julia exhibits less high spirits and more sensibility. She it is who compares the reuniting of Camitha Melton and her father to "Rousseau's picture of ... the meeting of St. Preux and Eloisa, after many years' absence." She is content to be as she is, despite the sufferings she experiences through sympathy:

But, like other people, I am inclined to hug my folly, if it is one; and had rather be dead, indeed, than dead to the lively sensations of love, friendship and gratitude.

In addition to the epistolary method, *Mount Henneth* recalls

Clarissa too in the brothel scenes, when an attempt is made to force the virtuous Camitha Melton into prostitution. Mrs. P——, the brothel-keeper, is realized with a little of the energy of Richardson's Mrs. Sinclair. When Henry Cheslyn offers £50 to secure Camitha's discharge, she replies:

> if I once can bring her to do business, and I have more ways than one, I can make two hundred of her the first month, and, before she is blown upon, sell her to some gouty lord for another.

The language has an unpleasant vigor, although Bage, who uses physical language very little, is quite incapable of backing it up with the visual effects so brilliantly used by Richardson. Nor does he attempt to explore the state of mind of the character in depth, preferring to move the plot along at a rapid pace.

Apart from Richardson, the other novelist whose influence may be discerned at least in parts of *Mount Henneth* is the Sterne of *A Sentimental Journey* (1763). In order to make the comparison, an episode which takes as its starting-point a famous scene in Sterne may be quoted at length. It occurs when Henry Cheslyn is searching for Camitha Melton:

> A few doors farther was a little milliner's shop; the mistress was leaning over the door. May'st thou, said I, be a relative of Stern's gentle Parisienne. I asked for gloves; she showed me a parcel; I took up a pair, and began trying them on. — They are too little, says she: — but I shall try, Madam; and rip it went in the instant. — Gentlemen are so boisterous, said she.
>
> And how do you fit your customers, Madam?
>
> By the eye, Sir.
>
> Then please to chuse me a pair.
>
> These, Sir, will fit you exactly. — They did.
>
> You have an excellent eye indeed, Madam; ten years ago, I fancy, it was a sparkling one.
>
> I thought so too, Sir, once; but a brilliant is little valued when set in lead.
>
> I presume it was in your power to have it set in gold?
>
> Yes, Sir, at the expense of a few other jewels which my silly grandmother taught me to set value on; but which seem to have sunk in the estimation of mankind, since my grandmother was young.
>
> Then of course they do not stand so high, as formerly, in your own esteem?

Much the same, Sir; only I have something less enthusiasm. Prejudices of education, you know, Sir, are difficult to be got rid of.

Then, it is probable that the ladies of that mansion have no grand-mothers?

I think otherwise, Sir, and that they find the remembrance of them grievous, when they are sober.

This is conjecture, I suppose; you can have no acquaintance within those sacred walls, because your grandmother brought you up in so different a religion.

She did not forbid me to sell ribbons or lace to the professors of any religion.

O charming! then you can, upon occasion, direct a stranger's choice to a deserving nun.

Pardon me, Sir; selling ribbons does not qualify me to judge of — merit.

You see, I suppose, many fresh faces, as well as handsome ones?

Yes, the succession is pretty quick; they are but a short-lived race.

It happens here, as in other nunneries, I presume, they are not all volunteers?

Mostly so, I believe. You gentlemen first seduce them from the protection of parents; and having treated them with a few months of fond rapture, your appetites jade, and all the rest is peevishness and ill-nature. The young creatures learn to drink, to drown reflection; you turn them out of doors, and they become — nuns, and please you, for bread. This is the ordinary process. Accidents, such as poverty, fraud, or violence, may bring reluctant ladies to — take the veil; but it seldom happens.

Have any of these fallen under your cognizance?

A few.

How does the worthy governess proceed with these refractories?

By two methods, temptation and terror. If the first fails, they are threatened with prison, which few have the fortitude to visit.

Did you ever know an instance of a woman of virtue betrayed here, who got out a woman of virtue still?

Never, unless I saw it this morning.

The relations between this scene and Yorick's encounter with the Grisset[20] is obvious: not only the setting and the situation, but the tone also derives from Sterne in its tentative, flirtatious humor. But the differences are highly significant. The whole purpose of the two narrators is radically different. Whereas Yorick wishes to prolong the situation for the sake of its suppressed sexual excitement, Cheslyn wishes tactfully to elicit information about Camitha. It is not a flirtation but a polite interrogation. The whole scene is given in dialogue, whereas Sterne uses direct comment to convey Yorick's actions and his feelings, on which the emphasis falls — the episode

justifies itself in the story because of the emotions to which it gives
rise. In the words of Henri Fluchère, "to Yorick sensation and the
emotion it unleashes are more important than the object that causes
them."[21] Bage, on the other hand, moves toward moral formula-
tions, as in the milliner's account of how women are led into prostitution by male callousness. Moreover, the episode is by no means
an end in itself; it leads the plot onward. The practicality of the
approach is emphasized by Cheslyn's later behavior; convinced of
the worth of the milliner, Mrs. Tyrrel, he helps her financially and
she eventually becomes a worthy older member of the Henneth
Castle community. The influence of Sterne is thus felt in the tone
and setting, but not in the main movement of the novel toward
moral explicitness. Fluchère has called *A Sentimental Journey*

a piece of sentimental rhetoric designed to bring people together better
than a sermon, in a communion of gentle emotions and generous
feelings.[22]

In *Mount Henneth* these emotions are complemented by an emphasis on common sense and rationality.

Mount Henneth attains its limited but real success as a coherent
criticism of late eighteenth-century English society. The best qualities of the novel are not those that link it to its English predecessors; Bage cannot match Richardson's psychological insight or
Fielding's control of comic-epic material. If Mr. Foston is of interest to the reader, it is not because of any particularity of realization.
He is a type of the rational benevolent man; his ideas, not his per-
sonality, are important. So, too, with many of the other characters,
especially the men. They are not distinct individuals attracting
interest in their own right, but parts of an overall pattern of
thought. Scott said that the novel exhibited "the strong mind, play-
ful fancy, liberal sentiments and extensive knowledge of the
author,"[23] and the emphasis is justified. In his general comments
on Bage's novels, Scott remarked that he was more concerned

to extend and infuse his own political and philosophical opinions, in which
a man of his character was no doubt sincere, than merely to amuse the
reader with the wonders or melt him with the sorrows of a fictitious tale.[24]

In this aim, Scott felt, he was nearer to Voltaire and Diderot than to
English writers: in addition,

the quaint, facetious, ironical style of this author seems to be copied from the lesser romances of the French school.[25]

Later critics have seen the justice of Scott's views. For instance, Miss Tompkins, in deploring the stagnation of the novel of the 1770s, states that Voltaire, although translated, was not then a significant influence, concluding that "even the *conte philosophique* had to wait for Bage before its seed became fertile in English ground."[26] In her opinion Bage brought to the novel "a great increase of intellectual content."

The question of French influence does not admit any definite conclusion, especially in relation to this early novel. F. C. Green argued in *Minuet* that thesis writers would be led by an abuse of the comparative method to stress too strongly the parallels between English and French literature of the eighteenth century; he denied that "the cosmopolitan spirit" left any "deep or lasting imprint upon the imaginative literature of eighteenth century France or England."[27] Nevertheless Voltaire's stories and Rousseau's romances were being translated[28] and often favorably received by reviewers and the public. Bage evidently knew the story of *La Nouvelle Heloïse,* at least sufficiently for Julia to compare the reunion of Camitha Melton and her father to that of St. Preux and Eloisa (Rousseau's Julie appeared as Eloisa in the early English translations). Several aspects of Rousseau's outlook can also be paralleled in *Mount Henneth* — hostility to dueling, contempt for polite society, the natural religion of the Vicaire Savoyard of *Emile.* Such sentiments were, however, the commonplaces of radical thought, and it is pertinent that in his thorough study of Rousseau's influence in England, Roddier invokes Voltaire in relation to Bage. Referring to the bringing together of a group of people for lively conversation, Roddier remarks:

[Bage] perfectionne le procédé, en donnant souvent à la discussion un tour dialogué, dramatique, à la manière de *Candide.*[29]

In tone, Bage is nearer to Voltaire than to Rousseau; his seriousness expresses itself in wit rather than rhetoric.

Like any other writer, Bage is eclectic. The epistolary form of the novels, with the contrasting female *confidantes,* descends from Richardson, and is also used by Rousseau; the comic characterization may owe something to Smollett; but in relation to the increase in "intellectual content" of Bage's novel compared with those of his English contemporaries, the example of Voltaire is also relevant, for his stories had demonstrated how unity could be achieved through a structure of ideas rather than the more usual emphasis in the novel on plot and character. Bage succeeds — in the wake of *Shenstone-Green* but with more energy and scope — in creating out of the heterogeneous material of the contemporary popular novel a modestly successful novel of ideas.

CHAPTER 3

Barham Downs:
Learning to Live in Society

*M*OUNT HENNETH derived its basic form from *Shenstone-Green*. The starting point for *Barham Downs*[1] was also provided by a novel (and indeed one also concerned with Shenstone), Richard Graves's *Columella; or, the Distressed Anchoret* (1779), which is directly referred to in an early letter. In the novel Graves amusingly criticized his friend Shenstone's Arcadianism. It tells of a young man who, in A. R. Humphrey's words, "after having been prepared by a liberal education, and a long and regular course of studies, for some learned and ingenious profession, retires in the vigour of life through mere indolence and love of ease, and spends his days in solitude and inactivity," and so "not only robs the community of a useful member in a more elevated sphere, but probably lays the foundations of his own infelicity."[2] This summary suggests features of the stories of both of Bage's Osborn brothers. He clearly found initial stimulation in his reading, though his novels cannot fairly be described as derivative, since they grow into something quite new.

Barham Downs was published in 1784 by G. Wilkie; its only republication was in Scott's selection for *Ballantyne's Novelist's Library* in 1824. The epistolary method is again employed, but with fewer correspondents. The most important of these are William Wyman, a sensible, active, and practical lawyer in London, and Mr. Davis (who is soon revealed as Henry Osmond), a young man of feeling who has retired from "the busy bustling world" to the "Elysian scene" of Barham Downs, to seek health and peace of mind. The novel is neatly organized, with the country village in the south of England providing its opening and closing scenes.

In between, Osmond learns that he cannot become a "hermit" at thirty-one. He has been jilted by the ambitious Lucy Strode, who

marries instead his elder brother, Sir George, a mathematician.
Osmond's initial reaction is to withdraw from the world, but he is
too sympathetic to others to be able to sustain his isolation. When
he learns that Lucy Strode has left his brother and eloped with Lord
Conollan, he is deeply distressed:

This quiet cottage, I vainly imagined, would have sheltered me from moral
as well as physical storms. No. Misery undeserved is the produce of the
plains, as well as peopled cities; and the sympathizing heart, to be totally
at ease, must have it's dwelling in the desert.

Similarly, his "sympathizing heart" is stirred by hearing about the
situation of the beautiful Annabella Whitaker, eldest daughter of a
wealthy, ambitious and empty-headed J.P., who is being courted by
the dissipated Lord Winterbottom, with her father's consent.
Nevertheless, Osmond's first reaction is to retire further from the
conflicts, to Switzerland, the country associated especially with
Rousseau's representation of the good life in *La Nouvelle Héloïse:*

I will go, says I, to a country of pure and simple manners. I will seek simplicity in the *paÿs de Vaud;* I will climb the rocks of Meillery; and, if I can
find the spot, I will live and die, where Julia lived and died; Julia Wolmar,
the most virtuous of her sex. I sketched, in my imagination, the face, the
features, of this lovely woman; but howsoever I began the portrait, the
End was — Annabella.

The solemnity of Osmond's concern ("if I can find the spot") and
the ineffectiveness of his efforts to find serenity in isolation are
neatly conveyed.
   Bage's awareness of the contemporary cult of the picturesque as
it affected literature is amusingly expressed in Henry Osmond's
letter from Sels:

   How often, in a fit of spleen, have I vituperated the whole race of land-
scape-drawing travellers, who interrupt their account of men and manners,
to describe what cannot be described so as to communicate an adequate
idea. With my eyes open, I am going to be guilty of the same impertinence.
Scenes "rush into my head, and I must write."

He goes on to offer one of Bage's few picturesque descriptions, of
Lausanne in its beautiful valley with river and lake. On the other
hand, Sir Ambrose Archer, writing from Montpelier, omits descrip-

tions of nature because "I shall cut a pitiful picture in it after the agreeable Mr. Moore." John Moore published *A View of Society and Manners in France, Switzerland and Germany* in 1779, and *A View of Society and Manners in Italy* in 1781. As these titles suggest, Moore's interest, like Bage's, was primarily in "men and manners," but he did not eschew picturesque description altogether.

The plot is largely concerned with Lord Winterbottom's attempts to carry off and marry Annabella against her will, and with Osmond's increasingly determined efforts to prevent this. In a highly melodramatic manner, the trail leads eventually to a secluded country house near Milan whose garden, like Barham Downs earlier, is described as "a perfect Elysium," but it is equipped for sensuality rather than virtue. The innocent Annabella comments with amusing incomprehension:

These grots are furnished with couches, and were, I suppose, intended for sleeping places in the most sultry hours of the day. And yet, why mirrors and naked pictures should be considered as incitements to sleep, I am unable to conceive.

She is rescued at the last decent moment. Other strands in the plot concern the relationships between Osmond's correspondent, Wyman, and Kitty Ross; and between Annabella's sister, the lively Peggy Whitaker, and Sir Ambrose Archer, a sensible squire. Thus the novel is brought, like its predecessor, to an idyllic end, with each pair happily married. At Barham Downs, as another correspondent puts it, all the virtues flourish: "Beauty without pride. Generosity without ostentation. Dignity without ceremony. And Honour without folly." The discriminations of value summarized here are enacted in the novel as a whole.

The plot of *Barham Downs* is derived from the Richardsonian novel of the pursuit of a virtuous female by a rakish male. Lord Winterbottom has no counterpart in *Mount Henneth,* and is rather a descendant of Lovelace in *Clarissa Harlowe.* But Bage's characterization is weak: Winterbottom, corrupt politician, accomplished seducer, and arrogant coward, is a mere villain. Bage has no psychological penetration: his moral insights are all social. The greatness of *Clarissa* lies in its presentation of the complex emotions of both heroine and villain; Clarissa and Lovelace are both caught up in passions which they cannot fully understand or control. At the heart of Lovelace's rant when he writes to Belford during Clarissa's final illness are bewilderment and anguish:

In fine, I am a most miserable being. Life is a burden to me. I would not bear it upon these terms for one week more, let what would be my lot; for already is there a hell begun in my own mind. Never more mention to me, let *her* or who will say it, the *prison* — I cannot bear it. May damnation seize quick the accursed woman who could set death upon taking that *large stride,* as the dear creature calls it! I had no hand in it! But her relations, her implacable relations, have done the business. All else would have been got over. Never persuade me but it would.[3]

Bage offers nothing comparable to this in Lord Winterbottom's obvious villainies.

In his study of Richardson, A. D. McKillop noted that after 1760 there was an increasing number of epistolary novels which derived their form from Richardson but expressed "a more trivial view of life than Richardson's."[4] He took as an example the anonymous *History of Wilhelmena Susannah Dormer* (1759), drawing the conclusion that "when the psychology has been subtracted from a Richardson plot, only sensationalism remains."[5] This raises the critical question about *Barham Downs:* what remains if there is no "psychology"? An answer is suggested by Bage's explicit reference to Richardson in the novel. When Annabella is in London she is taken to various entertainments, which, as a serious-minded girl, she finds vapid. These include, inevitably, Vauxhall, Ranelagh, and the Opera. She sees Benjamin Hoadley's *The Suspicious Husband,* in which Garrick was famous as the rake Ranger. But her reactions are unfashionable:

I believe scarce any character upon the stage takes with the ladies, so much as that agreeable rake, Ranger. The why of this is above my poor philosophy; but it is certain I incurred, all angel as I was, something like a sneer from two of the finest dressed gentlemen I ever saw, only for hinting a preference in favour of a Mr. Bevil, a Mr. Manly, and such out of the way people, because they were uniformly virtuous. Uniformity in goodness is uniformity in dullness, and the most uninteresting of all characters that ever were drawn is, I find, the stiff, starched, demure, formal ALL VIRTUOUS Sir Charles Grandison. This criticism was interrupted by the entertainment, a pantomime.... I yielded to the ridicule of the *tout ensemble,* and made merry with all my might.

In this passage the criticism is directed against the ladies and gentlemen who find it easier to admire vice than virtue. But it is the moralist of *Grandison* rather than the psychologist of *Clarissa* — to simplify the contrast for the sake of brevity — whom Annabella, here expressing Bage's view, admires. And what remains in *Barham Downs,* in the absence of "psychology," is a social and moral standpoint conveyed in an eventful plot and an assured, lively, and often amusing tone.

I *Scheme of Values*

The scheme of values is seen clearly in the parallel development of the Osmond brothers, both of whom modify an initial tendency to respond to life's problems by a deliberate turning away from them. The development, especially in Henry's case, is toward accepting social responsibility. At the beginning, his sensible friend Wyman thinks that Henry has been unmanned by his discovery of Lucy Strode's duplicity:

Has sensibility sunk thy spirit so low, that thou wilt bear to be robbed, insulted, laughed at? and suffer the inhuman pickpockets to wanton in thy spoils? Or hast thou delivered thyself over to the literal interpretation of thy bible book? and when a man takes thy cloak, givest him thy coat also?

The novel shows Henry accepting his responsibilities. When provoked by Lord Winterbottom, he ceases to be a quietist and writes him a vigorous challenge from the house of Sir Ambrose Archer, who is surprised by his vigor, as he tells Wyman:

The spirited letter he wrote Lord Winterbottom, he gave you a copy of. Though done in my house I never suspected the least circumstance of it; nor, to say truth, did I expect it from Osmond, who seemed to me to carry the virtues of meekness, patience and forbearance farther than the modes of the world will allow. These excellent christian virtues, I am sorry to think, are ill adapted to our gentility; or our gentility to them.

Wyman is in complete agreement with Archer about the necessity for virtue to be active. He replies:

Hermits and Monks will never possess my veneration; and a man who lives totally secluded from society, has my free leave to ascend to heaven, as soon as he is able.

Osmond must stay upon earth; he has virtues that adorn, and may amend society; and soon I think he will be called upon to act a distinguished part upon this theatre of human life.

The repudiation of withdrawal is emphatic. Bage also suggests that the emotional self-indulgence of the cult of sensibility may be hostile to the active attitude which renders help to those who need it. Wyman writes:

And yet, to feel imaginary distress, and to relieve real, may, for ought I know, be very different things. The first is become almost as fashionable with reading ladies and gentlemen, as dressing their hair.... Now I strongly suspect that too much familiarity with this sensation, may, in time, render *all* distresses imaginary, except one's own....

The tartness of the final phrase reveals Bage's sense of the need to "relieve real distress." In the course of the story, Osmond develops from being a sentimentalist prostrated by the news of Annabella's seduction to a man of action capable of going to her rescue.

The theme of social responsiveness is also treated in the story of Henry Osmond's elder brother, Sir George. He is a solitary student of mathematics, inveigled into marriage by the cunning of Lucy Strode,[6] who then deserts him for Lord Conollan, and ends unsuccessfully begging her husband for an increased allowance. Sir George develops more than any other character in the course of the novel. At first he is in poor health and low spirits, solitary and self-pitying. He tells Wyman:

I have shut up my heart against all the social affections; I have lived for myself alone, and what have I got by it? Hatred, Disease, Contempt, Money and Cuckoldom.

Later Sir George makes the generous act of sending £60,000 to his brother, and desires reconciliation with him. The brothers meet in Geneva, to their mutual delight; Sir George is anxious to be disabused of his earlier cynicism:

I have read in books, of Friendship, Benevolence, and other social affections, and thought it a pretty way of talking the world had got into, in order to keep the Love of Self, the sole efficient cause of motion in man, as much as possible behind the curtain.

Now the brothers ramble together on the Swiss mountains, examining the strata and enjoying each other's regard. By the end of the book, Sir George has become a good landlord, sending exact instructions to his bailiff about treating the tenants with generosity and charity. He has moved, as he says, from "the stoic apathy" toward "the social affections." The welcome he receives from the good-hearted bailiff on his return to England wins him further over to the "sensibilities." The final letter is from Sir George to an Italian friend, and it records his own change of outlook:

Thank heaven, this philosophy for a bear, is now done away; the pride of science has given way to the feelings of nature, and I am perfectly content to be pleased with what pleases other people.

The story of Sir George is thus a coherent development from solitary self-regard to feeling for others, which brings with it a felicity unknown to him before. Moreover, it is implied, other people will benefit from his restoration to humanity; the moping solitary benefits no one.

II *Social Criticism*

Thus *Barham Downs* gives prominence to the moral superiority of social activity over selfish withdrawal. But this does not in itself imply a radical attitude. The evidence of radical ideas is to be found rather in the faults portrayed in existing society and the alternatives suggested to them. Here the continuity with *Mount Henneth* is clear. Once again the upper class is attacked, this time through Lord Winterbottom's irresponsibility and immorality, and the readiness of Mr. Whitaker to sacrifice his daughter's happiness for a relationship with the aristocracy, as well as by more direct comment.

The condition of England, especially with respect to liberty, is discussed in a letter in which Wyman reports the remarks of a friend about two recent books, by the radical Dr. Richard Price and the conservative William Eden:

Dr. Price, a person of a pensive cast, who seldom laughs, says, He [Liberty] is still a child, and ricketty, and that the nation will go to the devil, for taking no better care of him. On the contrary, Mr. Eden says, he is as fine a youth as *need to be seen,* and the nation is a perfect paradise of wealth and happiness.... Dr. Price's book seems to me to have two unpardonable faults: Too much truth, and too little complaisance. Mr. Eden's corrects these errors, and may, not improperly perhaps, be compared to a garden full of the sweetest and finest flowers in the world, but with little or nothing to eat.[7]

This light tone is a successful vehicle for Bage's criticisms of the complacency of the ruling class. More direct political comment is given in an account of a meeting related by Sir Ambrose Archer:

I am returned from a meeting, called an association; the object of which is, as you know, to call upon parliament with a loud voice, to redress our grievances. And what are your grievances? says a well pensioned gentlemen, Mr. T'otherside. That the crown hath acquired too much influence by the worst of all possible ways — Corruption. That our representatives endanger their healths — by too long sitting. That as we never saw the least prospect of benefit, from engaging in the American war, we see as little from its continuance. Finally, That ministers carry their generous contempt of money, (public money we mean) into an extreme.

Here Bage gives an accurate summary of some of the main contentions of the County Associations which, developing from the example of Christopher Wyvill's Yorkshire Association, were active in several parts of England in the early 1780s. They brought pressure on the ministry to reduce taxes and to bring the war in America to an end. Although their policies were moderate, they contributed substantially to the criticism of the *status quo* and to the arousing of political concern.[8]

Further direct criticism of conservative attitudes is given by Wyman in an ironical account of the proceedings of the Ministry:

They have opened the historic page, and find in every leaf, that Wealth is the father of Luxury; Luxury the mother of corruption, and corruption, of political death. Wealth therefore is the grand object of their attack. If they can once get rid of this, real and nominal, they lay the axe to the root. Men will return to their primitive virtues, by the kindly aid of poverty; and what is of still more consequence at court, poverty is the natural parent of humility, and unmurmuring obedience. This being the case, can men go more directly to the point? When the Barons build again their castles, and restore mankind once more to the happy state of villenage, then will the learned monk tread the licentious page of freedom in the dirt, and give to truth and day, the deep-penetrating politics of these times.

As so often, Bage is at his best when most ironical; the ascription of improbable motives for the ministry's high taxation amusingly emphasizes the liberal values through the repudiation of medieval-ism. Another political scene occurs in London, when Annabella sees a satirical masquerade at the Pantheon. In it occurs a parody of ministerial language:

If mild and gentle influence has crept into this assembly, by what can mankind be better governed, than by mild and gentle influence? If it has gone forth into the nation, the nation will be so much the happier. It is of gothic barbarity to give it the harsh name of corruption.

The ministry has a majority of 201. Again Bage amusingly exposes one of the major political abuses of the time, the immense "in-fluence" exerted by the ministry, especially by John Robinson on behalf of Pitt.[9]

The most radical sentiments, however, are expressed through the Quaker doctor Isaac Arnold. He is a very sympathetic minor character, who is injured defending the young Kitty Ross from assault, and survives to be her friend and protector. When he is visited by Kitty's seducer, the Honourable Mr. Corrane, the follow-ing exchange occurs:

"Sir, you know my rank and situation in life" —

"I do," replies Arnold, "thou art the son of an Earl, and, I know not why, they call thee honourable."

"Is this treatment to be borne, Sir? I must inform you, Sir, I bear his Majesty's commission, and cannot put up with insult."

"Give me leave to inform thee in my turn, that I am Isaac Arnold, by birth a man, by religion a Quaker, taught to despise all titles that are not the marks of virtue; and of consequence — thine. I rank above thee."

This is lively democratic rhetoric: the Quaker disregard for titles neatly suggests the conflict of values with which Bage is so often concerned. A similar scene occurs later in the novel when Corrane's brother, Lord Cronnot, pays a visit to Arnold. The family wishes to ship Corrane off to America to save him from legal action for his kidnapping of Kitty. Arnold forces Lord Cronnot to compare this with his own recent treatment of the poor Perry Loggan, who had been hanged for stealing from Cronnot's granary when starving:

"Surely Mr. Arnold you cannot be serious in the comparison?"

"Why not, I pray thee?"

"Who the devil ever thought of uniting the idea of honour with the name of such a family?"

"The idea of honesty they may at least; as useful a quality amongst plebeians, as what thou callest honour amongst the nobility."

"But nobody talks at all of such people."

"Friend Cronnot, this may be the language of pride, but not of discernment. If thou art a Lord, the common people are men. Every class of life has *its peerage*. This Nobody of thine is nothing more than the bulk of mankind."

"Damn your sarcasm, Sir! Would it not raise the indignation of any man breathing to hear a fellow talk of hanging the son of an Earl for a little freedom with an insignificant girl?"

Thus Arnold enforces a radical criticism of the inequity of the law for rich and poor. But he also insists, in an equally radical spirit, that he does not wish to inflict punishment on Corrane for its own sake:

The only just ideas of punishment appear to me to be these. To deter the offender, and others also, from similar practices; and to spread the ignominy of evil deeds as far as possible, that they may be held in abhorrence, and may be cautions to the unwary. . . . I wish the young man good, not evil.

The treatment of Kitty Ross shows Bage's continuing dissent from the purely condemnatory attitude of society to the "fallen woman." Kitty, the daughter of a country doctor, is only sixteen when she is seduced. She is not represented as simply the passive victim of male sensuality, but as herself sensually aroused. After various adventures as melodramatic as those involving Annabella Whitaker, she is married by the shrewd Wyman. It is not in character for him to expatiate about his feelings, but his action in marrying the "fallen woman" (like Foston's in *Mount Henneth*) was a challenge to rigid moralists; like Mr. Foston's attitude to Caralia in *Mount Henneth* it aroused Scott's indignation in 1824.[10] This compassionate attitude is also shown in Sir George Osmond's instructions to his steward about a seduction on his estate:

The custom of society, punishes woman too much for this offence, and man too little. I will endeavour to correct this error. Let Yates [the possible seducer] look to it. Yet, if it be the fault of human fraility only, unattended with baseness or deceit, sour fanaticism might punish, but humanity must forgive. Comfort the poor girl in my name.

Charity triumphs over harsh convention.

The hostility to colonialism expressed in *Mount Henneth* with respect to both America and India finds less scope in a novel whose action is confined to Europe. But Bage's radical attitude is expressed by Sir George Osmond in a conversation with the Irish soldier O'Donnel, who has taken service in the French army because of English anti-Catholicism:

> "Well," says Sir George, "your country is going to recover her lost rights; America restores them to her."
>
> "And I thank her with all my soul; and I wish her good luck for it, by sea and land, and every other country too that deserves it. And what occasion is there for all this bullying and hectoring? and keeping one country in a dependance upon another? By my soul they will govern themselves well enough if you'll let them alone."
>
> "Well, we shall let them alone soon," replies Sir George; "Men will not be always under the empire of the moon."

After this generous and optimistic anticolonialism, it is a disappointment to find anti-Semitic feeling at the very end of the book. The bailiff's last letter to Sir George records this meeting with two Jews, creditors of the now dead Lord Winterbottom, Moses and Aaron Ishmagrock. They are referred to as "Israelites" and presented in crude caricature. The bailiff attacks their religion — "Your precepts are the puerilities of children" — and persuades them to drink with him. He claims that "two bottles more, and a hundred pounds a-piece, would have made them Christians." This unexpected lack of charity and tolerance is an exception to the pervasive liberalism, and suggests the depth of English anti-Semitism, but it cannot destroy the general sense that in this novel Bage is questioning many of the conventional assumptions and attitudes of his time.

III   *Toleration and Commerce*

In *Mount Henneth* the ideal of toleration was demonstrated in the growth of Mr. Foston's religious understanding. In *Barham Downs* toleration is emphasized in a number of ways. A conversation between Sir George Osmond the mathematician and Wyman the lawyer amusingly illustrated this; Sir George speaks first, criticizing his brother:

"How can you palliate his addiction to that most senseless study of poetry? What are the idle elegances of Virgil and Horace, to the manly wisdom of the divine Newton?"

"What are any of them, to Coke upon Littleton?"

"Hay, the devil! Where are we now, Mr. Counsellor? would you compare the pedantry of a profession, to liberal science?"

"No, Sir George; not to *liberal* science; all you have mentioned, and a thousand others, improve and adorn society. All are liberal, when they do not attempt to reign Lords paramount; and look down upon others."

Wyman's view is authoritative. Toward the end of the novel, the relationship between the scientific Sir George and an Italian professor gives the opportunity for further stress on toleration. In one conversation, Sir George denies that he is an atheist but claims that agnosticism is a rational point of view: men, like ants, have a limited capacity to understand their universe. The Italian is provoked:

"God bless me!" says the Professor, "this is such a monster of a comparison! I declare Sir George, you ought to be burnt for a heretic."

"Yes," replies Sir George, "it would tend very much to the glory of God indeed. Of all the insanities this busy, restless, insignificant animal, whom you dignify so highly, toileth and troubleth himself about, the most extraordinary, the most compleatly ridiculous, and most truly infernal, is that of making the brain of his neighbour vibrate exactly like his own, and of burning himself, if it does not."

The professor agrees that the Inquisition is an evil institution; he says that he would abolish it if he were Pope. The two men are firm friends despite their disagreements. They argue and make mutual concessions, "till they meet half way" on many issues. When the professor visits England, he is taken to Canterbury to see the cathedral but is not impressed by it:

"It looks," says the Professor, "this Canterbury Cathedral, as if it had been built for the *Dii inferni;* it is indeed a very solemn temple; and these fine brown antiques, which I suppose you dignify with the name of statues, were hewed, ready finished, out of the quarry, for expedition sake."

Sir George's lively reply accuses the professor of having no "taste for the awful; the sublime of this reverend pile." There is no attempt to show that one view is right and the other wrong. The conversational novel thrives on such differences of opinion, and the radical idea of toleration is emphasized.

From the 1770s onward toleration in its political sense was an important issue. As early as 1772 the Dissenting Application for guarantee of freedom from persecution was passed in the Commons, though rejected in the Lords. In 1779 the Toleration Act was slightly amended in favor of the Dissenters, but they now began to seek wider political rights through the repeal of the Test and Corporation Acts which restricted public office to Anglicans. Motions for repeal were introduced in the Commons in 1787 and 1789 (on which occasion it was defeated only by 122 to 102), and in 1790 (by which time anti-Radical feeling had grown strong in the country, and defeat was by 294 to 105). Toleration was one of the many victims of the increasing partisanship of the French Revolutionary period.[11]

It is true that Burke, the representative Conservative thinker of the time, supported the earlier requests for reform. But his reason for doing so was purely pragmatic, that persecution was against the interest of the state because it caused disaffection among the citizens.[12] He did not consider toleration as an ideal, which is a characteristic belief of the radical thinkers of the period. In his "Address to the People of Pennsylvania" in 1778, Paine wrote proudly of the contrast between England and America, where "we ... do not *grant* liberty of conscience as a *favour* but *confirm* it as a *right*."[13] And in the opening section of *The Age of Reason* (1794) Paine gave the rationale of toleration:

I do not mean by this declaration to condemn those who believe otherwise; they have the same right to their belief as I have to mine. But it is necessary to the happiness of man that he be mentally faithful to himself.[14]

The same spirit underlies Godwin's *Enquiry*. The whole of Book VI, indeed, is devoted to "Opinion Considered as a Subject of Political Instruction" and is directed against all forms of state control, as a corollary to his belief in the right and duty of private judgment. The exposition is full and lucid.[15]

As a novelist, Bage offers no exposition of the ideal of toleration, but he embodies it in dialogue and action. It even emerges unexpectedly in the treatment of dueling, a traditional aristocratic practice whose absurdity radical moralists often insisted on. In *Barham Downs,* the Irish soldier O'Donnel is an ardent duelist, although good-hearted and well-meaning.[16] Sir George Osmond, on the other hand, responds to the news of his wife's elopement with Lord Conollan in a "nonchivalric" way: "I am no fool of modern honour. Discovery, Divorce, and Damages, shall be my weapons of offence." The behavior of O'Donnel is absurd. He tells Sir George about a duel he fought with his friend Lord Conollan, explaining that he fired twice into the air. Sir George is ironical:

> "Was that the etiquette?"
> "It was the etiquette of humanity, my dear; for there was no occasion for me to kill him, without I had been killed myself."

O'Donnel is an inveterate duelist, and the savage Captain Wycherley dies fittingly at his hand after boasting of his assault on Kitty Ross. O'Donnel even fights another friend, Parry, over a woman in whom neither of them is really interested, and relates what occurred without self-pity:

> But Parry cleared himself like a man of honour, for he ran me through the body at the third pass; and the best swordsman in France could not have done it sooner. So I was satisfied; and if I had not I should have been quite unreasonable.

Finally, Parry visits O'Donnel and they discuss their behavior in an amusing piece of dialogue:

> "What was it to you, O'Donnel, that I amused myself with a willing woman? You had refused her, you know?"
> "But she was Lady Osmond," says I; "the wife of my friend, and I would as soon resent an affront done to him, as to myself, and sooner too."
> "And how", says Parry, "did Sir George behave to you upon a similar occasion?"
> "By my soul, like a noble gentleman — like a man of sense — Not like a man of modern fashion — Like a fool — Like a blockhead."
> "O'Donnel, if his sentiments are right — yours are wrong."
> "Oh, the devil burn me," says I, "and why can't they be both right? and what is right or wrong at all but what a man thinks to be so?"

Thus Bage indicates simultaneously the absurdity of the code of honor to which the duel belongs, and the belief in tolerance as a more rational ideal.

A final topic which is brought forward in *Barham Downs* is that of the relationship among commerce, progress, and contentment. In *Mount Henneth,* several stories suggested the demoralizing effects of the effort to rise in the world, implying an ideal of quiet acceptance. In *Barham Downs* this ideal still appears, for example in the account given by Henry Osmond of his idyllic life in the Swiss village of Sels:

The house I live in was given in charge to a gardener, and a very pretty young woman his wife. Simplicity and innocence appear in all her actions. She is my chambermaid, and performs the duties of that office, not with the bold effrontery of an English chambermaid at an inn, but with an unapprehensive modesty.

The tranquillity of the village is defended by the wise and benevolent Pastor. He preaches a sermon on human frailty which leads the villagers to decide against the establishment of a coffee and wine house, with its latent possibilities of corruption. This is very much in the spirit of Rousseau's *La Nouvelle Héloïse,* as F. C. Green's comment on that novel suggests:

The really eloquent pages of his letters are those which express enthusiasm for the antique simplicity and primitive goodness of the Valaisans, and his dreams of perfect married bliss, with Julie, amongst these kindly, happy, mountain folk.[17]

In England the situation is quite different, and, Bage sometimes implies, morally worse. For instance, Sir George Osmond writes in commendation to his bailiff for proceeding leniently with tenants in arrears with payment of rent, seeing the tenants' behavior as all too natural in the circumstances:

It has happened in a land of commerce, that riches have been diffused, and that the occupiers of land have come in for a share. It has happened also that they have shared a part of the corruption of manners which riches also introduce. No doubt they are prouder, more self important, more sumptuous. And how should it be otherwise, since they are men? Amongst what body of people, whose wealth was increasing, have they had better examples?

Nevertheless, as was seen in the earlier discussion of the political themes of the novel, Bage also ridicules the idea of going back, under the Tory ministry, to "the happy state of villenage."

Lois Whitney, in her thorough study of eighteenth-century primitivism, notices Bage's indecisiveness on this point, which helped to convince her "anew of the futility of even looking for a consistent system of thought in the pages of a popular novel."[18] But it is the coexistence of contrasting ideas in Bage's novels which make them novels of ideas rather than novels of doctrine. In this instance, the issue is complicated, and even the question as to which attitude is the radical one cannot be answered unequivocally. Many radicals were optimistic about the effects of commerce in creating a more flexible kind of society, while at the same time their ideal community (as can be seen in Rousseau) was often small and uncompetitive. Most radical philosophies, indeed, contain both the impulse to dynamic change and the suggestion of tranquillity at the end of the road. Bage dislikes the false social ideal of luxury and the alternative of regression to feudalism, but his indecisiveness is within a range of radical ideas.

The influence of Graves, Richardson, and Rousseau can be discerned in *Barham Downs,* the first two in the plot and the last especially in the Swiss scenes. But the main positive quality of the novel, its coherent expression of a radical view of society, is not derived from any one source, for the tone is again nearer to Voltaire than to Rousseau. In *Barham Downs* there is clumsiness and melodrama, but there is also a thoughtful concern about society, and a lively treatment of current problems in dialogue as well as exposition, which marks it out from most contemporary novels as the product, if not of a born novelist, at least of an intelligent mind.

CHAPTER 4

The Fair Syrian:
National Manners Compared

$\mathbf{B}$AGE continued to use the epistolary form for his next two
novels, *The Fair Syrian* (1787) and *James Wallace* (1788). The
former received the most favorable review Bage had so far had, in
the *Monthly Review* for April 1787.[1] A pirated edition appeared
in Dublin in the same year, and a French translation in Paris in
1788.[2] Recently, however, it has become very rare indeed — it is
impossible to locate a copy of either English edition in the British
Isles.[3] Nor have recent critical comments brought out the interest of
the novel. J. R. Foster, who pointed out that the most exotic elements of the plot derive from Prévost's *Histoire d'une Grecque
moderne,* in which the virtuous Théophée is sold into an Oriental
harem, also remarked that *The Fair Syrian* showed Bage's sympathy for the French people.[4] But what is important is that, if Bage
is sympathetic to the French people, he is decidedly hostile to
French institutions. Professor Steeves has praised the novel as
"moving upon a higher plane of both characterization and characteristic humor" than its predecessors, but also remarked of it,
"Structurally, it is the most rambling of them all; the plot, the most
improbable."[5] While it is true that the plot is improbable and occa-
sionally confusing, the structure of the novel is more closely related
to its theme than such a criticism allows.

The action of the novel certainly has a wide geographical range.
It opens in 1781 with a young French aristocrat, the Marquis de St.
Claur, on his way to join Rochambeau and the American forces
fighting against the English. St. Claur is captured by an English
officer, Captain John Amington, whom he comes to admire for his
integrity and self-control. Amington is disillusioned with the war,
and is glad that the Americans win. The two young men become

73

friends and visit various parts of America together. They then return to England, where Amington becomes Sir John on his father's death. His sister, a vivacious wit, has married Lord Bembridge, who is devoted to horse-racing and the gaming table. St. Claur and Sir John visit Ireland, where both fall in love, St. Claur with a simple Irish girl, Aurelia Clare (whom he saves from her boorish cousin), and Sir John with Honoria Warren (whom he saves from a murder charge framed against her). In both cases the social stations are incompatible. St. Claur returns to Paris, where he finds himself bored by fashionable life and under pressure from his formidable mother to marry a woman of her choice. Thus ends the first volume.

In the second, Honoria Warren tells her story, which provides the exotic element in the novel: she had lived in the East and been sold into a harem, though her virginity had been remarkably preserved. She spends some time at Lady Bembridge's, but leaves eventually because of Lord Bembridge's attentions. Meanwhile, St. Claur flies to the Levant to avoid the arranged marriage. He finds himself suddenly imprisoned in Constantinople, and an elderly English fellow prisoner turns out, in true romance style, to be Mr. Warren, Honoria's father. The two men are soon freed and they eventually come to Sir John's country house. Lord Bembridge has by now fallen deeply in debt and left the country, and a sensible Scot, Lord Konkeith, has appeared. As usual, the novel ends with marriages — Sir John and Honoria, St. Claur and Aurelia; Lady Bembridge and Mr. Warren complete the group, which Konkeith also plans to join. The final letter tells of the friends' plan to divide their time between France and England, while St. Claur will reorganize his estate in Normandy along the lines of Sir John's in Hertfordshire.

I   National Contrasts: America, France, Turkey

The Fair Syrian resembles Bage's earlier novels in its relaxed tone, and in its movement through various complications to the establishment of a small group of sympathetic characters aspiring to live together responsibly and contentedly. It has a wider geographical range, which, although partly serving to provide exotic color, is also worked into a pattern of ideas. For, in a simple way, Bage is making a comparison of national manners and so suggesting his own radical view of what constitutes the good society.

A major contrast is created between American simplicity and

French sophistication. St. Claur finds "the saints of Boston" rigid and unsympathetic, though he is able to extract some amusement from their habits:

They received me well, and talked to me of Jesus Christ, John Calvin, the Devil and the damned English. Those who did me the honour to invite me to dinner, always carried me to church, as a preparative. The saints find devotion a hungry business.

Here the feeling of the novel is perhaps with St. Claur, but he soon finds himself out-argued by a sturdy Quaker farmer in Pennsylvania, who forcefully contrasts the lives of the peasants of France and America to demonstrate the superiority of the American way of life:

In France, how poor they are! how abject! starving in the midst of those delicious delicacies they are daily creating, as it were, for the use of others. . . . View the same rank in America and acknowledge the difference. It would be insulting thy understanding to point it out. Every man feels himself a MAN; claims his share of the common bounties of nature; and, above all, of liberty. It is true, you have a vast superiority in your trinketmen, your *tailleurs, perfumeurs,* your *perruquiers,* and *cuisiniers;* and may a thousand ages elapse, before America becomes your rival.

(The modern reader may feel that history has dealt ironically with this prayer.) The Quaker goes on to attack the grand Monarque, and then the Catholic Church:

In my youth, I also read tragedies, epic poems, romances and divinity. Now I read COMMON SENSE.[6] And what pretty epithets hast thou adapted to the dignity of the sacred order? Wilt thou not think we are given over to all uncleanness of spirit, living as we do un-sprinkled, dying un-unctioned. Can there be salvation, thinkst thou without a bishop? Without that order of men so useful to a nation that chuses to think by proxy? But to tell thee a secret and it may serve to confirm the differences in species, American heads are so pertinaceously constructed, that rather than not take their own road to heaven, they will take none at all.

The self-righteous note is nicely sustained. However, when St. Claur defends the Church, the Quaker comments, "Thou art right. Education is all in all"; the differing backgrounds, it is implied, account for the differing views of the two men. The Quaker nevertheless goes on authoritatively to attack the French aristocracy —

"an order of *fainéants*" — and the French attitude to love: "Our guide is nature, and the laws of society. Yours, fashion and sentiment." The contrast is borne out somewhat painfully for St. Claur when his advances to a Congress General's wife in Philadelphia are met by a smack on the face; Puritan America repudiates sophisticated France. St. Claur writes ruefully to his friend St. Flos thanking Heaven that in France, "though we have not the love of liberty these ultra-Atlantics boast, we have the liberty of love, which to a Frenchman is all the liberty worth a *Louis d'or*." But he admits to doubting whether these "liberal opinions" are likely to promote "harmony domestic": he may even appear "a coxcomb of magnitude" in his friend's eyes.

Certainly on his return to Europe St. Claur no longer behaves in the conventional way of the French aristocrat, although his mother the Marquise tries to force him to do so. He treats Aurelia Clare in a manner more American than French, and his ideal is based largely on the English country gentleman. He is well aware that Aurelia is not the kind of girl with whom a Frenchman would be expected to fall in love: she knows nothing "except praying and pudding-making, and such grandmotherly goodnesses." St. Claur is forced to return to Paris on the command of his mother, who keeps him still "trammelled in the swaddling cloaths" of her financial control. He finds that he has been called back to defend his sister's honor from the advances of his friend St. Flos. It later becomes clear that the Marquise had encouraged the affair until it seemed likely to interfere with her daughter's proposed marriage to an elderly rich widower, and that it was no more in St. Flos's eyes than the "simple unmeaning gallantry" expected of a young man in Paris. Nevertheless, a duel is fought, St. Flos injured, and St. Claur deeply upset. After St. Flos's recovery the two young men become the closest of friends again, but the whole affair suggests the absurdity of fashionable French life and manners.

America, on the other hand, for all its people's lack of flexibility and humor, is seen as the land of freedom and self-reliance. John Amington's feelings change radically while he is in America. Having enlisted enthusiastically, he ends with strong pro-American sentiments:

Fatal to half the world would have been the hour in which we had enslaved America. — Most fatal to ourselves. Happy, that the nature of the country, the independent spirit of the greater part of its inhabitants, and our unsettled councils, have combined to render the design, if it was design, abortive.

A similar attitude affected the well-known contemporary English radical Major John Cartwright, who refused to take part in naval action against America on conscientious grounds in 1776.

Although the action of the novel does not return to America, the radical values of the Quaker farmer remain as part of its pattern of ideas. The same moral, extended to cover India as well as America, is expressed by St. Flos in condemning English arrogance to Sir John:

Yes, you are a free nation, and hate despotism most vigorously, when yourselves are not the despots. The East groans under you still; so would the West have done, but that it chose to fight rather than groan.

Through St. Flos Bage expresses his radical view of colonialism.

In contrast, the Marquise's plans for her son's future suggest the falsity of French values; she promises St. Claur that she can secure his promotion, in either the army or the church, by her influence. He, however, has learned a different ideal from Sir John, that of unpretentious social utility as a country gentleman:

I would get me a pretty little wife, and we would make pretty little children, and love them, and one another. And I would make two blades of corn and of grass where only one grew before, which the English philosophers say is quite as useful an employment as murdering mankind....[7] Now as I have no ambition for a general's batoon — no holy aspirations towards a crozier, and a perfect indifference for blue or green ribbons — what can I do better than double the value of my estate in the country, and be useful to my neighbours?

The Marquise taunts him with having the feeble ambition "to yawn life away in the woods of Caux" with Aurelia Clare, "a mere country girl, known to nobody," and tries to force him to marry a partner of her choice. To avoid this, St. Claur leaves France. Before he does so, however, he witnesses the launching of the Montgolfiers' balloon:

Seventeen Academicians, with telescopes and micrometers, of the best construction, were appointed to watch the motions of the aerostatic *ignis fatuus*. A thousand flags were waving in the air to note the course of the wind.

St. Claur sees the scene as emblematical of the French tempera-
ment, with its preeminence in superficialities. Now the French have
proved their "volatile essences." Thus Bage gives the Montgolfiers'
famous exploit of 1783[8] an emblematical significance, fitting in
well with his overall pattern of ideas.

One of the liveliest conversations in the novel, between the formidable Marquise and Sir John, brings out the contrast between
French and English attitudes in a different spirit from that of
Burke. Sir John continues the line of argument of the Pennsylvanian Quaker about freedom of thought:

> "If you debar yourself the liberty of thinking, how will you distinguish
> prejudice from truth?"
> "Liberty of thinking, Sir! We think in France, as well as you in
> England; only not so licentiously perhaps; nor do I see why our modes of
> thought are to be called prejudices, more than yours."
> "Nor I neither, Madam, unless when they profess to have been derived,
> and not to have undergone our own examination."
> "When we profess to derive them, Sir, we take care of our authorities;
> whilst you, thoughtless English men, follow no authority, except of those
> *ignes fatui,* your own deluded imaginations."
> "It is true, we pay little regard to any authority, but of nature, reason
> and our laws, none of which, I confess, have a just claim to infallibility,
> when men are interpreters. Undoubtedly the Pope by divine right is far
> above them all; but he is at a great distance, Madam: you cannot have him
> upon every emergency; would it be therefore amiss in some cases at least,
> to know how to do without him."
> "You are pleasant, Sir; but heretical jokes will never convince me I am
> wrong."

The success of this and similar conversations in Bage is that both
parties are allowed vigor and determination. But Sir John is able to
conclude with a flourish, in speaking of Miss Clare:

> "She appears indeed to hold family pride in tolerably just contempt."
> "In *just* contempt! I infer from this that you, Chevalier Amington, have
> no family to boast."
> "Not much indeed. We trace, I suppose, from some scoundrel Norman
> in the suite of William the Conqueror; but I have never been at the trouble
> of looking over the roll."

Bage allows his hero to have it both ways, being an aristocrat and
speaking democratically. But Sir John fails to convince the Mar-

quise, despite his appeal as "an untutored son of nature, who has seen too little of the world — and Paris." The values of Paris are shown as thoroughly corrupt. The contrast between Mr. Warren's relations with his daughter and the Marquise's with her son emphasizes this. St. Claur's last reflections about his mother, after her death, include the realization of how his French attitudes have been influenced and changed. He could not accept the "principle of submission," he says, because he had learned differently "in the thirteen provinces, and amongst you licentious Americo-Angles of the old-world." The reeducation of St. Claur emphasizes the falsity of French values, with their concern for outward show and their lack of rational foundation.

While the contrast between democratic America and aristocratic France is essential to the structure of *The Fair Syrian,* the third prominent area, the Ottoman Empire, is used mainly to provide exotic elements. The Oriental romance was indeed a popular literary form in the eighteenth century; Beckford's *Vathek* (in Henley's translation) had appeared in 1786.[9] On the whole Bage relies on the interest of the exotic, and presents the Orientals sardonically. For instance, the rich Syrian who buys Honoria at Bosra is described as typical of his countrymen:

To smoak tobacco with aromatics, to drink coffee, to chew opium, and repose upon a sofa, were the regular occupations of the day. Add to these, luxurious suppers, wine, and women; and you have every thing a Turk thinks of value upon earth.

His death from an overdose of "provocatives" in preparation for bedding a new slave is no more than poetic justice. The Syrians' attitude can be seen more seriously, however, as an extreme form of the French devotion to superficialities. Its political result is a corrupt system of government in which arbitrary power is unchecked. Honoria and her father, and later St. Claur, are victims of arbitrary power which coexists with large-scale corruption. Even the Divan, or high court, it is suggested, is open to bribery. The arbitrary rule of the Porte is shown to be incompatible with rational values, and this is equally true of the Russian system: the Czarina is described as "the greatest bully in petticoats amongst the princes of the earth." Bage's hostility to authoritarianism is consistent.

II   *England, the Two Traditions*

If America and France (with Turkey) indicate the two poles of
social thought in the novel, England might be expected to represent
the norm. This is true in the sense that St. Claur is won over to Sir
John's outlook on life, but there is also a sustained contrast among
the English characters themselves. Against the rational Sir John
(who nevertheless is prevented for long from marrying Honoria
because of her social inferiority) is set the gambler and rake, Lord
Bembridge. The liveliest female character in the novel is Lady Bembridge, who expresses, with an intelligence of which her husband is
incapable, the conventional view of how the upper classes should
live. She chides her brother, Sir John, for his eccentric idealism:

Lord Bembridge's fortune and quality place him amongst the folk of
rank and fashion. Now the folk of rank and fashion frequent Newmarket,
fight cocks, build, plant, game and run in debt; and must my spirited lord
be debarred the priviledges of nobility, only because he did you the honour
to marry your sister?
   . . . But then you would have him harangue the house upon the dignity
and integrity of past times; and oppose the court; and make protests:
Waste the midnight lamp in projects for the country's good; banish luxury,
taste, and fashion; build churches, or endow an hospital; and restore the
reign of miracles and mince-pyes. Dear Brother, banish these whims; come
amongst us, and enjoy your five senses. Do as other people do.

This is a vigorous defense of the manners of the upper class; Lady
Bembridge is always fluent and amusing. But the terms of her final
appeal — "Do as other people do" — reveal the basic emptiness of
the values she is defending. It becomes clear that she is making the
best she can of the position into which she is married, seeing the
choice as being "a woman of fashion — or a martyr." Lady Bembridge takes her brother to task again for excessive hostility to
pleasure:

My dear Sir John, your philosophy is too gloomy. I believe you call it the
Stoic. But Epicurus, they tell me, was quite as wise a man as Zeno. Put
money in your purse, brother; and come and tread paths far removed from
the haunts of spleen. . . .

He replies, denying that he is a "penurious rustic, a sour cynic, or a
canting methodist." He is not hostile to pleasure, but believes that

it must not become "the business of life," and he is deeply afraid of the evil influence of gambling, to which Lord Bembridge is addicted.

Lady Bembridge receives Honoria Warren into her household at her brother's request, and the debate is continued between the two ladies. Lady Bembridge writes to Sir John, giving her own vivacious impression of Honoria: she is beautiful and learned, she can paint, play music, and speak four languages, but she does not play cards and is thus unsuitable for high society:

In short, Sir John, if you intend to marry and settle in the country; the Duke of Wharton's grand curse upon the dog that bit him; if you intend to live a life of perfect tranquility and sleep; there is not a woman on earth so capable of giving you this vegetable happiness. As to her possessing any of those respectable qualities, which serve to advance a husband's interest, or render him *conspicuous* in the great world — No.

The sum of it is, that she is fit for nothing, but to make you happy. So take her at your peril.

This passage is very open in its irony. It presents two alternative ways of life, the fashionable and the domestic, and leaves the decision to Sir John. His position is parallel to that of his friend St. Claur, except that while the latter had to resist the demands of his powerful mother, Sir John's conflict is inward. An old servant puts the situation clearly to him:

To be sure, as the world goes, she is not a fit wife for you, Sir; but if goodness was greatness, I don't know who might not be proud to have her.

Sir John admits to his correspondent Osborne that although he felt that Honoria would make him an ideal wife, he was led by pride at the thought of marrying a poor woman who had been in prison to make "cursed proposals" to her. Thus in the course of the story Sir John learns that character is more important than rank, a moral which might be found in the romance tradition but which in Bage is part of his radical social thinking.

Lady Bembridge tries to keep a balance, by means of irony, in her attitude to the society into which she has married. She suggests that Honoria might also compromise: "Condescend to be a Venus at night, and I will allow you to be a Minerva in the morning." But compromise proves impossible. Lord Bembridge makes advances to Honoria, and plans to establish her in Bartlett-square in place of his present mistress, Nancy Somes, "a delicious girl, but expensive." Honoria leaves the house and takes rooms on her own. Finally it becomes clear that Lord Bembridge has incurred so many debts that he will have to take refuge abroad. Lady Bembridge will stay with her brother and "set the uncommon example of a fine lady returning to the shades for happiness, and finding it there." Thus it becomes clear that her defense of fashionable society was a matter of self-defense rather than conviction; her feelings lead her gladly back from the fashionable to the simple life.

The ideal to which the novel moves is clearly expressed in St. Claur's plan for his future activities as a landowner:

I have ten thousand acres of land to clear, and to drain. I have also three hundred *paysans* and as many *paysannes* who live in cabins, and who wear wooden shoes.... Politicians may say what they will, but a constitution of government which gave this three quarters of mankind a few of the comforts of life, would be a good constitution. Man to be sure is a god-like animal, but he has one dog-like property, that of eating his mess, bones and all, hiding the overplus if he has any, snarling all the while, and sometimes biting the poor hungry devils who dare to look up at him with an eye of humble desire ... in ten years I hope to see my peasants as plump and almost as saucy as the English peasants, who are as much of the latter as can be desired.

In this way Bage holds up the ideal of responsible social activity embodied in the traditional English country-gentleman. Such an ideal links Bage to Fielding's Allworthy and Smollett's Matthew Bramble, and so suggests a conservative rather than a radical standpoint, but the same ideal appealed to thinkers of the French Enlightenment, like Voltaire, as representative of a better order. Moreover, the country gentry had played a leading part in the activities of the County Associations in the early 1780s and their influence was by no means simply conservative. What is clear is that Bage's ideals derive from the English tradition as much as from his wider reading.

III   *Sexual Morality and Ethical Individualism*

The treatment of sexual morality in *The Fair Syrian* is again bold. In Prévost's novel based on the true story of a Circassian slave, Aissa, brought from Constantinople to France by the French Ambassador, M. de Ferreol, Théophée resists all the blandishments by which he attempts to persuade her to become his mistress.[10] At first Bage follows this. When Sir John, slightly drunk, suggests that Honoria should become his mistress, since her rank prevents her from becoming his wife, she indignantly refuses. But when Sir John falls into fever as a result of his rejection, Honoria comes to him and offers to become his mistress — though with a self-sacrificial dignity which makes him repent of the suggestion. She is greatly relieved by his refusal, but the initial offer of herself has a boldness unknown to conventional fiction at the time. Professor Steeves has perceptively discussed this scene as showing Bage's use of argument "not to affront conventional susceptibilities, but to encourage better understanding of the obscurer grounds for the moral sanctions."[11] The institution of marriage is thus brought under scrutiny before being reasserted.

Honoria's behavior was influenced by her meeting with the slave-girl Amina, who taught her to make the best of life even in the harem. Amina's father was a Christian noble of Teflis in Georgia, who fell suddenly under the displeasure of the Porte. She tells Honoria:

I knew nothing of the matter, but that the great Sophy sent for his head to Spahawn, and the governor of Georgia was so good as to take care of his estates, and to hang up all the males of the family.

The tone of this is close to Voltaire, a master of the Oriental tale to whom Bage is clearly indebted both for this part of the story and more widely in his general approach.[12] Amina has reconciled herself to slavery, and argues that many sorrows are created by their sufferers. At first Honoria prefers "the sensibility that pains me" to Amina's "unfeeling merriment." She is disturbed even to think of their moral position in the harem:

"The idea fills me with horror. I prefer death a thousand times."
"And I prefer a thousand times — to death."

Honoria's conventional morality sounds rhetorical set against this prudential realism; it is not surprising that this novel was not reprinted by Sir Walter Scott. Honoria admits that she was influenced by her unconventional companion (a predecessor of the golden-hearted prostitute of later fiction):

Thus did the wild, untutored, sensible madcap turn, and laugh at my most serious arguments. She was, however, one of the best natured creatures in the world; always entertaining, and always disposed to oblige; and I must confess my philosophy not a little indebted to her.

Such an influence offered a challenge to conventional sexual morality.

Finally there is a discussion of marriage between Sir John (who is about to marry Honoria), Lady Bembridge (whose husband's creditors are closing in), and Lord Konkeith (a rational commentator). Sir John defends marriage in a solemn tone which curiously anticipates Scott's when denouncing Bage's sexual morality in 1824:

"...No laws, no decorums of society, are more important than those which relate to marriage; nor can the community be more hurt, than by a looseness of principle in this great particular."

"And so, Sir John, would you have Lady Bembridge torment herself for life, just to shew the world the goodness of her principles? The world would laugh, as I do, when the strong indelible laws of nature are ordered to move in subservience to the punctilios of society. Every creature seeks its own happiness; and who will deny its right, when it has missed it in one path, to seek it in another."

"Not I, my lord. Nor did I mean to contend against a sister's happiness."

In accordance with this radical view of marriage, it is decided to seek an absolute separation for Lady Bembridge from her husband. His death in a duel renders this unnecessary, but Bage has challenged the conventional idea of the duration of marriage. Thus the handling of sexual morality in the novel is in a questioning spirit, although the happy ending is as usual brought about by marriages.

The central idea of *The Fair Syrian* may be the active and useful country-gentleman, but it is flanked by the more radical suggestions of the Pennsylvanian Quaker and, in a different spirit, the slave-girl Amina. The novel moves away from Fielding and Smollett in its insistence that behavior must be based not on tradition but on the individual's moral decisions. As Honoria writes to Sir John, "What else can, what else ought, to be the guide of my actions?" And a letter from Lord Konkeith at the end of the novel draws attention to the fact that the group which he is thinking of coming down from Scotland to join — Honoria, Mr. Warren, St.

Claur, Sir John, Aurelia, Lady Bembridge — consists of people who refuse to behave according to the stereotype of their class or country:

> I have taken an unaccountable liking to the whole group, and a pretty group it is! A female slave from Asia, possessed with violent notions about chastity and the holy trinity — A merchant busy for half a century amassing wealth where-ever he could find it, content at last without accounts of debtor and creditor. A gentleman from France not caring a sou either for absolute monarchy or transsubstantiation — an Englishman hating cards and horse races and unconditional submission — a wild Irish woman, gentle as a lamb — a beauty and a wit taken from the great world to the shades without dying of grief — and "though last not least in our dear love," a rough highlander, seeking England without hopes of getting money in it! One, two, three — ay, seven; seven wonders. But the eighth would be that seven such perverted heads collected from all the corners of the earth should live a fortnight together without quarrelling. We shall see.

Bage's heroes and heroines are not typical of their countries; they are independent, free-thinking individuals.

Lord Konkeith is, like Dr. Gordon in *Mount Henneth,* a Scotsman of probity and intelligence. Like Sir John, he fought in America and became disillusioned with the English cause. Honoria describes him favorably:

> Lord Konkeith, Aurelia, is a middle-aged gentleman, very poor for a Lord, which is not an uncommon thing; but to be at once a Scotchman, poor and independent, borders, according to certain drawers of caricature, upon the miraculous. He has, it seems, other ill qualities; as a passion for truth, a turn for satire, a contempt for frivolity of every species, and an intrepidity which carries him directly to his point.

Bage resists the caricaturist's tendency to oversimplify national types. Konkeith is a sympathetic character for Bage because of his seriousness and directness.

In his criticism of upper-class society, Bage is more successful in *The Fair Syrian* than in *Barham Downs* insofar as Lord Bembridge is better drawn than Lord Winterbottom. His vices are less extravagant and more convincing. The idealism of Sir John and Lord Konkeith is attractively conveyed, but it is notable that these embodiments of a more radical attitude to life both have inherited titles. Bage perhaps feels some inconsistency in this acceptance of a common romance tradition of titled heroes which has no connection with radical sentiments. At all events, he allows Mr. Warren to express a radical view even after his daughter has married Sir John. Lady Bembridge records the conversation:

"If a man has been eminently serviceable to his country and appears at court with a star on his breast and a garter round his knee, we acknowledge that he deserves the distinction; but we cannot think that the son of this man, happening to have been begot by him, rather than by another, on this account is entitled to get above us."

... "But, my dear Sir," said Honoria, with an affectionate glance at my brother, "men of rank may have enlarged and liberal minds."

"Why then let the respect be paid to their minds: I am willing every mind should be respected in proportion to its value; men of family, and men of no family, would then be nearer upon a level than is generally allowed."

Bage does not go so far as, say, Paine was to go in *The Rights of Man* in welcoming the abolition of all titles in France: "Titles are but nicknames, and all nicknames are titles."[13] But he effectively questions the hereditary assumption.

The Fair Syrian is a consistently genial novel. Despite the geographical wanderings, the central concern about the good society is explored throughout and focused at the end. If the characterization is sometimes weak (it is difficult to distinguish Honoria from Aurelia, for example) and the interpolated tales overly long, this is compensated for by the lively play of argument, especially with such characters as Lady Bembridge, the Marquise, and Amina. There is much of Voltaire in the book, not only in the Oriental episodes but also in the criticism of French society, the hatred of arbitrary power, the belief in free thinking. But the radical assumptions of the Enlightenment emerge, rather unexpectedly, embodied in an English country-gentleman, to replace the superficialities and affectations of the French aristocratic code. The novel shows clearly how Bage's social criticism, however it may have been clarified and sharpened by French influence, arose from a tradition of English social thought.

CHAPTER 5

James Wallace:
The Middle-class Assertion

J AMES WALLACE was published in 1788,[1] a year later than
The Fair Syrian, and received a mixed reception from the
reviewers.[2] Its only republication was by Scott in *Ballantyne's Novelist's Library* in 1824. The complications of the plot, especially
those concerning the mystery surrounding the birth of the epony-
mous hero, occupy a good deal of the reader's attention. But again
there is lively social observation and comment which helps to make
it a sane and interesting work. And in the choice of some of the central characters, specifically drawn from the commercial classes,
James Wallace clarifies Bage's position as a critic of society.

The novel begins with the correspondence between Paracelsus
Holman, the son of a surly pharmacist and his harshly orthodox
wife, and James Wallace, an orphan brought up by Mr. Holman.
Paracelsus is blunt, Wallace polite, but both hold unconventional
social views. Wallace is soon in trouble for supporting a Mr.
Thomas Garridge against the son of Sir William Saxby at a cricket
match, and is dismissed by the lawyer for whom he works for
"effrontery" in refusing to apologize. The elder Mr. Garridge gives
Wallace a position as his clerk, but his unresponsiveness to the
unattractive daughter, and his refusal to marry the servant girl who
has been seduced by the son Thomas, cause him to be sent away.
He sets up as a lawyer in Carlisle, but runs into debt through
extravagance, is imprisoned, and on his liberation goes off to the
Continent with the rakish Mr. Scovel; he is again imprisoned, set
free by the efforts of a passing young Englishman, James
Lamounde, and sent back to Liverpool to take service with
Lamounde's sister Judith, in the house of her uncle Paul and his
sister Rebecca. The profusion of incident allows little scope for the

development of Wallace as a character, although his career does contrast with the more practical activities of his friend Holman.

Through a second pair of correspondents, Judith Lamounde and a school-friend, Pauline Edwards, the story is continued. Judith tells of a new friend, Caroline Thurl, and her boorish brother Havelley, who has proposed to her and been rejected. Judith has had to make use of the services of James Wallace to protect her from her suitor's unwanted attentions. Wallace is a favorite with Judith's guardian, Paul Lamounde, a Liverpool merchant who conceals his benevolence under a gruff manner. Judith visits the Thurls at their home, where she is courted by Sir Antony Havelly, *savant* and fop, until he is frightened off by the warnings of his cousin Havelley Thurl. On her return to Liverpool, Judith finds that Wallace has been slightly injured in a duel. He is so overcome on seeing her that he places his arm around her waist, simultaneously apologizing for the freedom. Discovering the strength of his feeling for her (and to avoid the advances of her elderly aunt), Wallace leaves the Lamoundes and embarks on a sea voyage on a trading vessel. An interpolated story concerns the ship's Scots Captain, Patrick Islay, a virtuous and successful trader.

The next section is one of the few in Bage which can be said to achieve suspense. It concerns Pauline, an orphan brought up by a humane clergyman called Edwards, and Sir Everard Moreton, a former pupil of Mr. Edwards, an attractive young rake, and friend of James Lamounde. A letter from Pauline to Judith about Sir Everard's attention to her, and his suggestion that she should accompany his mother and himself to Westmorland, is followed by an exultant letter from Everard to James about his plan to trap Pauline: "A wife, Lamounde, for affairs of state; but for affairs, not of state, a maid — a maid." When James pleads with him not to carry through the plan, Everard reproaches him as being like a preacher at Moorfields or the Tabernacle, but "Divine Crebillon! thou art my master now."[3] Soon after this James leaves for Westmorland, and the next letter is from Paracelsus Holman at Allington to Paul Lamounde (whom he has never met), telling him that James and Sir Everard have been injured in a supposed quarrel, and are now at Holman's house. Sir Everard had in fact shot James and then himself, and Pauline's honor had been saved. Like most eighteenth-century fictional duelists, both James and Sir Everard recover, but unlike, say, Clifford in John Moore's *Mordaunt*

(1800),[4] Sir Everard does not abjure his rakish ways but remains interestingly himself.

The effect of the duel is, however, to clarify the whole plot. It brings Judith to Allington, where she learns of Wallace's devotion and delicacy. But Wallace himself is now in Spain, and soon becomes a victim of the arbitrary powers exercised in that country. Lady Moreton is struck by the story of the orphan Pauline, who had been left with the Reverend Mr. Edwards with a letter from the mother to an unnamed sister. When the letter is brought, in true romance tradition, Lady Moreton realizes that *she* is the sister, and the dead father was Wallace Islay, the brother of the trader Patrick. Moreover, Pauline has a brother, born at Allington in Lancashire, namely James Wallace. The mystery is thus cleared up, and the way is clear for a happy ending.

Sir Everard, characteristically, finds Pauline less attractive now that she is likely to become his wife, and goes off to London in search of distraction. Alone, Judith sits in a romantically gloomy spot reading Wallace's letters, until the sudden arrival of Caroline, James, and Wallace himself, conveniently freed from his Spanish imprisonment. Love is rapidly confessed and the two appropriate marriages arranged. The novel, as is usual with Bage, does not close with these individual marriages, but with the establishment of a "neighbourhood". James invites Holman, whose practical good sense impressed them all at Allington, to come and join them in Liverpool:

Ten merchant families agree to give you five hundred pounds per annum to take care of their household. I will answer for your success.

Lady Moreton, too, would like to come and live nearby. Sir Patrick Islay (as the Captain has now become) is also to join the party. Holman is keen to be there, as he indicates to Wallace (now Islay):

Give me notice when you shall be at Liverpool: I fly to you instantly. I accept Mr. Lamounde's kind offer, and will live and die among you.

In this way, the novel follows its predecessors in concluding with the establishment of a small community including the main characters.

James Wallace differs notably from the earlier novels, however, in that there is one major figure who remains obstinately unneighborly. Sir Everard is now in Paris, and James writes to him there regretting his "voluntary exile." Just previously Sir Everard has responded with vigor to James's criticisms of his course of life:

You, on the contrary, learnt the astronomy of virtue from those, I suppose, who learned it of John Calvin, at Geneva, that crab-faced fellow who burnt Servetus, because Servetus was not quite so sour as himself. Instruct me, dear James, what are the signs of justification and grace? Can a man know, with any tolerable certainty, if he be, or be not, one of the elect?

And it is Sir Everard who has the last word in the novel, mocking the idea of a permanently happy marriage. He thinks of his companions in Paris and contrasts them with James's group:

Debauchees and sharpers! good Captain Fanbrook! Tolerably illustrious too, some of them, for birth and family. In the grace of God I believe they are not equal to the upright commerciants of Liverpool; nor do they get up matrimony so sweetly: But for the manufactures of wit, mirth and good-humour — I doubt the abilities of your artists must fall short; and curse me if I don't prefer these looms to those for the weaving of saints....

The police of Paris will have no occasion to animadvert upon me for many years. When they do, depend upon it I shall prefer their Tyburn, the Greve, to the charity and contempt of friends and relations.

Kind Preceptor, Yours...

No other eighteenth-century novel gives its last words to an unrepentant rake. The unexpectedness of it brings liveliness to the conclusion, and throws into relief the contrary values of "the upright commerciants of Liverpool" which have been defined and upheld by the total movement of the novel.

I   Critical Views

As J. R. Foster has indicated, there are a number of parallels between *James Wallace* and Smollett's *Humphry Clinker:*[5] both concern young men of mysterious origin who find employment as footmen, and both have as important characters — Paul Lamounde and Matthew Bramble respectively — elderly men who conceal their sympathetic natures by an irascible manner. The type has been well described by T. R. Preston as "the good-natured misanthrope,"[6] in whom we can observe "an ironic tension between speculative misanthropy and actual good deeds."[7] Other examples of this type given by Preston are Samuel Sarcastic in *Shenstone-Green,* Sir Howell Henneth in *Mount Henneth,* and Wyman in *Barham Downs,* but Paul Lamounde is the most fully developed instance.[8] A conversation between Lamounde and James Wallace reveals their basically similar, although superficially contrasted, attitudes; Wallace wishes to enlist his employer's help for the distressed Mr. and Mrs. Dorrington:

"And so, Sir, you would really have me undertake the cause of these silly people?"

"I own I wish it, Sir."

"To rob folly of its proper reward; you mention the man's genius and learning: Sir, they are his peculiar condemnation. Pretty qualities, to waste in idleness and vanities!"

"Their folly has been great, Sir; so has been their punishment. For a few cups of honey, they have long drank the waters of bitterness. The innocent children too, Sir — !"

"And are punished for the sins of their Fathers. That is a divine ordinance, and you would counteract it."

"I would, indeed, Sir."

"When you go about to divert the ordinary course of human affairs, how do you know but you are creating more future evil, than you are doing present good? You remember Zadig."

"The conduct of an angel, who can see into futurity, may be directed with certainty to the greatest good. Men can only be guided by what they know. I am sure, Sir, that it is no maxim of yours, that no one ought to attempt a probable and proximate good, for fear of producing a remote and improbable evil."

"No, Sir — but man is an ass — these remote and improbable evils are upon his right-hand and upon his left, whilst the fool, guided by passion or prejudice, will only look strait forward."

"Passion, Sir, and prejudice, I hope, are not the general guides to charity, compassion and benevolence."

"I hate the cant of benevolence; books are full of it; it fills our mouth, and sometimes gets as far as the eye, but never reaches the heart."

"Not never, Sir."

"What is it at best, but the ostentation of vanity?"

"Not at *best,* Sir; that can hardly be allowed to be the motive of a man, who is pleased to do good, and pleased to conceal it."

"If there be any such, the man is ashamed of his folly, perhaps."

"These are sentiments, Sir, which issue from the mouth, and are contradicted by the feelings of the heart. Will you have the goodness to pardon, me, Sir, if I suspect your assumed principles ill agree with your practice?''

"Practice, Sir! Does any man accuse me of these milky doings?''

"Some men, Sir, and some women. If all gratitude were as strong as Mrs. Calthorpe's, you would not be able to do good by stealth.''

Bage's dialogue is characteristically lively here, and the emphasis is neatly thrown on the idea, shared by the two men, by which "the cant of benevolence" goes further than "the sympathetic tear" of the sentimentalists, and translates itself into action. Both men know Voltaire's *Zadig,*[9] but repudiate its moral, that human beings should rely on Providence rather than try to shape their own futures. Thus the parallels between *James Wallace* and *Humphry Clinker* certainly exist, but they do not determine either the form of Bage's novel (which does not follow Smollett's use of the journey as a unifying device) or its pattern of ideas. For although both novelists may exalt true benevolence, Smollett does so through the traditional figure of the country-gentleman, with a strong nostalgia for simpler times, while Bage's ideal is associated with "the upright commerciants of Liverpool," representatives of the rising trading classes at one of the developing provincial centers. This emphasis also distinguishes *James Wallace* from *The Fair Syrian.*

Bage's regard for the values of the trading classes is expressed in several ways in the novel. Most directly it is embodied in Paul Lamounde himself, the descendant of a Huguenot family who combines benevolence with business sense. The family spirit is expressed also through Paul's brother, especially in his death-bed advice to his children. He tells his son James:

With regard to your future avocation I leave you free; you may be a gentleman with an independent fortune. I should rather advise you to be a merchant, and increase it; but do not regard the gain of the profession as your sole inducement. You are affluent; every day presents a benevolent merchant opportunity to benefit some worthy man. Do not withhold the loan from the unfortunate, nor suffer merit to sink under distress.

To his daughter Judith the dying man gives advice about choosing a husband, which indicates his good sense and distrust of merely social values:

Make it a habit to examine the source of your sensations, especially of the tender kind; are they excited by beauty of person, of dress, or address? These are trifling causes, and never act, except for an instant, but upon trifling minds. Your favourite poet has said everything in these two lines: —

> Worth makes the man, and want of it the fellow;
> The rest is all but leather — or prunella.
> Thus My dear Judith — Worth makes the man.[10]

These radical sentiments emerge naturally from the social situation of the class to which the Lamoundes belong.

A similar point of view is expressed through the story of Patrick Islay, the Scots captain who befriends James Wallace. He is the son of Sir Wallace Islay of Cromartie, an impoverished chief who is conscious of his rank and despises commerce. He thus stipulates that his youngest son, Patrick, shall have a traditional education, although he is to become a merchant. Patrick comments sardonically:

> So I learned latin and mathematics, and read history auld and new: But with aw my learning, I naver could ken how exchanging the goods of one nation for those of another, and benefiting baith by the operation, could damage my blude.

One can sympathize with Scott's authoritative comment:

> his Scotchmen are awkward caricatures, and the language which he puts in their mouths, not similar to any that has been spoken since the days of Babel.[11]

But Patrick Islay offers a further example of the self-reliant trader, and is a suitable friend for Paul Lamounde and member of the Liverpool community.

Scott went on, surprisingly, to assert that Bage's chief power lay in his ability to detect "the internal working of a powerful understanding, like that of Paracelsus Holman." He is certainly one of Bage's most striking creations, a strong-minded, practical man of a scientific cast of mind. His father, a surly pharmacist, had carried his scientific enthusiasm to absurd limits. His attempt to restore some clover by diffusing salt through a stack led to a fire, but he still went on to follow a French idea, about which he had read, of improving his land by electrifying the fruit trees: this cost him £70. It has been suggested by M. Vitoux that Bage is here referring to some of Priestley's ideas about the practical application of electricity, and felt to be surprising that Bage, an enthusiast for new ideas and attitudes, should satirize the elder Holman.[12] But this is consistent with Bage's Swiftian preference for the practical over the "projected." Mr. Holman is a candidate for the Grand Academy of Lagado; his enthusiasm never produces any substantial benefits. Paracelsus (characteristically christened thus "out of pure venera- tion for that great physician and chemist")[13] is no less dedicated to science, but he is also a man of practical good sense. When he is left a legacy, he invests it in a glass-works:

Of myself I have little to say, except that I have purchased a fourth share in a neighbouring glass-house[14] with my aunt's £2000, which is to be turned into an half, whenever I can leave Allington and my present busi- ness, to bestow my undivided attention upon the conduct and improve- ment of this manufactory.

This project links Holman to Dr. Gordon in *Mount Henneth,* an- other practical idealist, but Holman is the more fully developed character. His social views are determined and radical, as can be seen in a brief letter to his friend Wallace when the latter is in trouble for having assaulted the son of Sir William Saxby:

This is a very awful business, James Wallace, this beating the son of a Baronet. It is breaking the first great tie of subordination, and introducing confusion amongst the ranks of society. You will be made sensible of this, no doubt, at the Hall, and brought back to your character of easy com- pliance. I tremble with impatience, Wallace. If thou hast bowed down to these strange gods, thou art an idolater, unworthy of the land of liberty, unworthy the friendship of

                                    PARACELSUS HOLMAN

Holman is outspokenly skeptical about many social conventions and attitudes. His behavior is often eccentric in his total rejection of the ideal of gentlemanly self-control. Judith describes his display of emotion on hearing the news of James Wallace's birth:

The man was mad with joy. I think he kissed me about twenty times, hugged my brother, and shook my uncle's arm almost out of joint. He danced, capered, prayed a little, and swore much; till at length a Spanish jail coming into his head, he almost burst into tears, and hurried out of the room.

Toward the end of this novel, Lady Moreton expresses her admira- tion of his outspokenness:

I am much pleased to find that you have a design of engaging Mr. Holman
amongst you. Besides his skill, his conversation is extremely entertaining;
and when your uncle and he are together, I think, I hear again the strong
masculine sense so common when I was young; but which appears to me to
be almost lost in the insipidity of modern politeness.

Through Holman is rejected the artificial code of behavior of the
upper classes, and in its stead is presented the radical idea of a man
of forthrightness and integrity who is valued on his achievement
and abilities rather than on his manner and rank.

II *Criticism of Society*

Criticism of the manners and attitudes of the upper classes is
expressed in the satirical treatment of several characters. These
include the contrasting figures of the boorish squire, Havelley
Thurl, and his foppish cousin, Sir Antony Havelley. Judith
Lamounde reports the latter's affected response to his French
valet's informing him that he must prepare for dinner:

> "Lard! says Sir Antony — at three! dine at three!
> What a sacrifice to consanguinity am I necessitated to make!"

He is an amusing character, in the tradition leading from the
Restoration fops to Peacock's Mr. Listless, set off against the rustic
manners of his cousin:

> Grace being said, Miss Thurl enquired of Monsieur Tuissele what wine
> his master drank?
> *"Toujours le claret, Madame."*
> "Blood, says the 'squire, it will rot your guts out, cousin; but come —
> let's have a bumper to Church and King."
> "The politer nations, says Sir Antony, have laid aside the custom of
> drinking toasts."
> "Why so? — says the 'squire — it's hearty, and promotes good fellow-
> ship."
> "There are, Sir, who think it blunts the nice sensibility of the nerves,
> and consequently destroys the finer affections."
> "Finer affections! What be those? By George, I'm never more loving
> than in my cups."

The conversation is again lively and amusing, as each character
exposes himself in turn. But it is Sir Antony's affectation which is

the main focus of the satire. He is *savant* as well as dandy, and in this capacity he has cultivated the habit of abstraction, so that his answers to questions are sometimes misdirected. Judith Lamounde writes:

After several questions, therefore, asked by Miss Thurl, which produced monosyllabic replies, or none at all, I ventured to ask his opinion of the Italian ladies. Sir Antony took the mien of considering the question profoundly; and, after a minute's pause, answered, with great politeness, they are viviparous, Madam ... Spalawzani, ladies, continued he, has observed several parturitions.[15]

He explains that he thought the question was about

the *simiae volantes,* an African animal, which has lately been the subject of investigation in Italy; the learned cannot determine whether it is bird or monkey.

Sir Antony is the antithesis of Paracelsus Holman; he is a dilettante (like the Caradocs in *Mount Henneth*) with no idea of making use of his knowledge to benefit humanity. He is, by his own account, a "fellow, *speciali gratia,* of no less than three foreign academies of science, as also of our illustrious royal society at home." Wendeborn, in his account of England, noted that the Royal Society was often criticized (in his view, unfairly):

It has been said, that many of its members became such merely from vanity; and that they are admitted only on account of their payments, though they have, as it is pretended, no claim either to learning or taste.[16]

Sir Antony has plenty of vanity, though he has at least some learning, too. He wishes to marry Judith Lamounde, but she rejects him with a full sense of the class distinction between them, as is obvious from the conversation with her uncle Paul:

"He's of a new order of coxcombs. I have never seen any before who joined foppery to science."
"I am told the conjunction is common at Paris."
"And this is the first importation. Prithee, Judith, which of his fine qualities art thou captivated with?"
"Women, my dear uncle, seldom fall in love with learning; but Sir Antony, as you must needs see, has a charming taste in dress; then you cannot but remark how genteel he is."

"Yes — if it be ungenteel to have a carcase of flesh and blood."

"Then his pensive, gentlemanlike air, uncle. — And his title; is it for the daughter of a simple merchant to resist so many attractions?"

Again a lively conversation emphasizes the criticism, from a middle-class point of view, of the externality and emptiness of upper-class manners. When Sir Antony speaks to Judith herself, he is astonished to find that she is unimpressed by his birth, rank, and fortune, and refers with disgust to the rumor that she has preferred a footman — "a rival who would be honoured by his cane." Judith replies indignantly:

I allow the sublimity of these ideas, Sir Antony; but must beg leave to interrupt their course, in order to rectify an error into which you have fallen, by supposing the accomplished Miss Lamounde must be blind to merit, because it has neither title, nor coat of the loom of Lyons.

With such radical rhetoric she dismisses Sir Antony.

The representatives of the upper classes in the novel are "placed" in various ways. Sir Antony is absurd in his complacency and affectation, while Sir Everard Moreton, unrepentant to the end, is Bage's most convincing rake because of the vigor with which he expresses his repudiation of respectability. Havelley Thurl is of the lesser country gentry, and is treated less severely, although his boorishness is not disguised. He is, as Judith Lamounde notes, a throwback to the coarser manners of the earlier part of the century:

At the beginning of this century England was supposed to contain twenty thousand country 'squires, "whose laughs were hearty, though their jokes were coarse," who devoted themselves to the cellar and the chace....

It is said, that in the course of the last twenty years this race has entirely disappeared, and divines, and philosophers, as usual, wrangle about the cause. The first ascribe it clearly to the mild influence of the Christian religion; the other to the influence of wealth upon manners. A penetrating lady here assures me they are both wrong, and that this great and remarkable event is wholly owing to the beneficent race of barbers and hairdressers.

The question of social progress, of the correct balance between integrity and refinement, is amusingly raised. Later, James Lamounde contrasts Havelley Thurl favorably with Sir Antony:

I allow, indeed, that Mr. Thurl's exterior manners are not so polished as
the present age requires; but Miss Thurl will be so good to remember, that,
under an exterior much more unpolished, our ancestors had to boast of a
manliness of action, and a generosity of spirit and sentiment, which, I
fear, are incompatible with the refinements Sir Antony seems to have
adopted.

James himself remains fastidious, and does not reply to Havelley's
invitation to "come and see Moll Parkins — a fine crummy
wench." But the idea that refinement can go too far is suggested
again later, when Judith explains to Pauline why the conversation
of gentlefolk is so often vacuous:

> ...conversation — I don't mean talk, my dear — is not the fashion.
>   My uncle remembers well when it was so;...
>   But then, it must be owned, there was sometimes a horrible clash of
> opinion in very good company, especially when religion or politics were
> the subject; the two grand sources of disputation. By degrees it became the
> fashion never to introduce those spoilers of peace; and hence we are said to
> have now a most gentleman-like religion, never offensive by exuberance of
> zeal, and a most accommodating public spirit, perfectly acquiescent in
> every measure of every minister. In short, the good English people, with
> some exceptions, choose rather to be ignorant and polite, than learned and
> contentious. So far, my uncle.

The tranquillity of eighteenth-century England depended on the
establishment of a consensus, and consensus always involves the
likelihood of vacuity. Bage is hostile to a tranquillity based on the
Chesterfieldian negatives;[17] he prefers the forthrightness of Paul
Lamounde and Paracelsus Holman. But there is also the suggestion
in such younger characters as James Lamounde and James Wallace
Islay himself that the improvement of manners need not necessarily
lead to moral and intellectual decline, so long as it is combined with
a life of useful social activity. The possibilities of human nature are
not exhausted by such upper-class types as the rake, the fop, and
the boor.

III   *Commerce*

In *James Wallace,* therefore, although there is little direct political reference, there is strong class feeling: a radical hostility to the
upper classes is the counterpart of commitment to "the upright

commerciants of Liverpool." Even in Spain, where James Wallace
is for a time imprisoned, it is the "respectable merchants" who
come to court, pity him, and rejoice in his release. The traditional
idea of social superiority based on rank is challenged by a radical
idea of social utility. It is true that Bage goes with the romance
tradition still to the extent of discovering his hero to have the noble
blood of the Islays, but he also allows Paracelsus Holman to comment ironically:

A title too! Why even philosophers allow it to be an agreeable play-thing,
if one may give the name of a noun-substantive to a thing that can neither
be seen nor felt. No man ever despised it, say they who have it, except the
man who has it not. Faith, I believe they are right. Not to have some predi-
lection for distinction and pre-eminence, is above the virtue of man, when
man is polished and refined.

Well then! it shall have its play-thing, please God, its uncle — and
myself.

Here provincial good sense asserts itself against the romance tradition in an amusing way; "when man is polished and refined,"
which Holman emphatically is not, he may value titles highly, but
otherwise he will see them as "playthings." Throughout the novel
Bage endorses the values of the commercial middle class to which
he belongs, enforcing a radical criticism of society. The "upright
commerciants of Liverpool" are the counterparts of the merchants
of Birmingham, like Bage's friend William Hutton and the proprietor of the Soho Works, Matthew Boulton. It is fitting that the most
distinguished scientist of the Lunar Society, Priestley, should be
referred to by name and with respect, although in a humorous context, early in the novel. Mr. Holman is told by a doctor that the
French will use balloons as secret weapons in a future war against
England, and that they will be filled with the "inflammable air"
discovered by Priestley. Paracelsus goes on:

Here ended the Doctor's relation, and my Father has thought more about
it than about my Mother ever since. He fears the consequences for his dear
country, and is debating whether, as a dutiful subject, he ought not to
advertise government, and advise the taking Dr. Priestly up; more especially as the Doctor is a traitor to the Church as well as State, as appears
evidently by his polemics, and by his tracts in favour of Dissenters, and for
repealing the Test and Corporation Acts; for though my father has his
heterodoxies in matters of faith, he is well convinced that the Church is the
grand pillar of the State.

Priestley's radicalism was well known, and Bage makes clear the source of his own values by this reference; *James Wallace* is his most overt expression of belief in the middle-class radicalism which was so noticeable in the Birmingham area. His positives are science and commerce, self-reliance and social utility.

M. Hazard devotes a chapter of his *European Thought in the Eighteenth Century* to "Natural Science," emphasizing how widespread and eager was the interest in scientific knowledge:

> You only had to give a cursory glance around you to see signs of an unmistable effervescence. Everywhere the *curiosi* were getting down to work.[18]

In his chapter on "The Encyclopaedia," M. Hazard shows how important a position the writers of the Enlightenment gave to machines, and to those who invented and used them. This meant a new evaluation of human activities:

> Empiricism demanded a transference of dignity, and it now passed from the sphere of speculation to the sphere of the practical; from thought to action; from the head to the hand. Diderot, in espousing the cause of the mechanical arts, was true to his doctrine, to the ideas he shared with his brethren, to the philosophy of his age.[19]

The parallel development in England is described by A. R. Humphreys in *The Augustan World* in the chapter "The World of Business":

> The prestige of the practical life brought into the limelight a new kind of person, shown at its best by Wedgwood and by Matthew Boulton.[20]

Adam Smith's *Wealth of Nations* (1776) is said to embody this attitude in its "humanity of style and tone."[21] Bage welcomed the development in his novels, and most explicitly in *James Wallace*.

The middle two novels show Bage developing. In *The Fair Syrian* he increased his range by the comparison of different social systems, and in *James Wallace* he made more precise his view of the English social classes. But he was still hampered by the epistolary form. This was never particularly appropriate for his undertaking, which involved neither Richardson's psychological probing nor Smollett's humorous characterization, but rather a concern with social ideas. Thus it is not surprising that Bage abandoned the epistolary form after 1788, and that his last two, and best, novels were written in the freer manner which this allowed. G. F. Singer, in his study of *The Epistolary Novel,* remarks that Bage stands out for the humor of his writing in a genre often handled sentimentally, and also praises the characterization of his correspondents,[22] but notes a paradox in his use of the form for social criticism:

It is interesting to observe that, despite the fact that these novels of Bage are written in letters, the epistolary novels wane with the vogue for works of just the social type Bage tried to write.[23]

This view of the relation between form and theme is confirmed by F. G. Black; the epistolary novel declined as the Gothic novel and the novel of social purpose developed, and was less fashionable in the 1790s.[24] Bage began writing in the form that came most readily to hand, but abandoned it as his skill as a writer matured. In his last two novels the ideas are expressed with the greater clarity made possible by his increasing maturity as a writer.

CHAPTER 6

Man as He Is:
The Establishment Challenged

I N 1792 William Lane published *Man as He Is,* Bage's fifth
novel, at the Minerva Press. In it Bage abandoned the epistolary
technique and achieved greater unity of plot and theme. The title
belonged to a contemporary fashion. A comedy by Mrs. Inchbald,
performed in 1788, had been called *Such Things Are,* and later in
her career she was to produce the drama *Wives as They Were*
(1797). Eliza Parsons published *Woman as She Should Be: or, the
Memoirs of Mrs. Menville* in 1793; Godwin entitled his best novel,
Things as They Are; or, the Adventures of Caleb Williams in 1794.
Mary Anne Hanway followed with *Ellinor, or the World as It Is* in
1795, and Bage called his last novel *Hermsprong; or, Man as He Is
Not* in 1796.[1] This fashion suggests the background for a well-
known witticism of Charles Lamb's recorded by Hazlitt:

It was at Godwin's that I met him with Holcroft and Coleridge, where
they were disputing fiercely which was the best — Man as he was, or Man
as he is to be. "Give me," says Lamb, "Man as he is *not* to be." This saying was the beginning of a friendship which I believe still continues.[2]

Man as He Is begins with an amusing preface, in which Bage
refers to the popularity of the didactic novel in England:

To a refined and sensible people, — says Mr. Rousseau, — instruction
can only be offered in form of a novel. The English are a refined and sensible people; and I desire to instruct them in the best manner possible.
Indeed, the mode of instruction by novels, is become as prevalent as Mr.
Rousseau himself could have wished; and, to all who think in his elegant
manner, will be irrefragable proof of my beloved country being, what-

soever may become of our politics, the first of nations, for refinement and sensibility.[3]

But the reviewers, Bage argues, are nevertheless hostile to the novel, either because Le Sage, Marivaux, Fielding, and Smollett have no worthy successors, or because the novel is believed to corrupt good manners. The reading habit is now widely spread, especially among women:

It is not now — as in the days of the good Queen Ann — when none read, but those who could read. Except the wives and daughters of country labourers, all women read now, or seem to read.

Finally, Bage reports the critical response of a "lady of taste" to whom he had shown the novel:

"You call it a novel," answered she. "No, sir — it is not a novel. A novel should have plot. You have no plot. Character — but character is not your forte. Incident — you have indeed a few small incidents, but weak, and by no means of the right sort. Of the marvellous — nothing. Of distress — why you have absolutely no distress that deserves the name. And for love! — oh, I promise you, your twenty thousand fair readers will not thank you for the lessons you have given them on that subject."

Having thus warned the reader that he does not intend to supply the stock popular novel of romance, marvels, and distress, Bage leaves it to the reviewers to decide "WHAT IT IS."

Bage, no longer using the epistolary method, feels it necessary to assert in an Exordium that what follows is a "true history" extracted from "certain papers," showing "that a deviation from virtue is a deviation from happiness." Fortunately this moral is conveyed with characteristic vivacity in the story of the young George Paradyne. He is the well-meaning and amiable son of an excellent landowner, Sir Jeffrey Paradyne, who is drowned, together with his eldest son, at the start of the novel. His widow, Lady Mary, contrasts with her late husband; she "had little fortune, and was therefore under the necessity of setting a very high value upon rank." George has a lively sister, Emilia. The novel is constructed upon the simple tug-of-war principle, with Sir George having to choose between a life of selfish pleasure (to which he is directed by his mother and her brother, Lord Auschamp) and a life of affection and responsibility (to which he is directed by his uncle and guardian James Paradyne — "a plain country gentleman, and an honest, though not perhaps very sagacious, justice of the peace" — and his tutor, Mr. Lindsay).

On a visit to Hampshire, Sir George and Lindsay meet Cornelia Colerain, a sweet girl who has been cheated by a rejected suitor of the fortune left by her merchant father, and Miss Carlill, a witty and assertive young Quaker. Sir George falls in love with Miss Colerain, and has romantic dreams: "she called for his assistance in a thousand dangers; he flew, he swam, he dived, he fought to save her." But she thinks that he is too young, and she too poor, for it to be right for him to propose, and goes away with her faithful maid and Negro servant. Just before this, and while slightly inebriated, he visits her and behaves with more freedom than she can allow. His behavior is criticized by Miss Carlill, who tells him, indicating a central theme of the novel, that he is not a "gentleman" but "only a man of birth and fortune." Meanwhile, his sister Emilia has become engaged to a middle-aged, wealthy, proud Anglo-Indian, thinking it "better to be Mr. Birimport's wife than Lady Mary's daughter."

Away from Miss Colerain, Sir George soon declines further from the ideal of the gentleman. He meets an old Oxford acquaintance, John Lake Fielding, who has recently inherited £40,000 and who introduces him to the social life of London. Sir George meets Lady Ann Brixworth, a fashionable beauty who encourages him, admitting him "to the early part of her toilette, before she was visible to the admiring world." He also gambles a good deal with Count Colliano of Turin and the Marquis de Valines in Dauphiné, as well as making friends with the gay and humorous Lt. Harcourt. But he has not yet been converted by London, Fielding and Lady Ann from "a man into — a man of mode." He is still torn between the two ways of life open to him:

> If he sipped of animation at Weltjie's, Minerva, in the shape of Lindsay, would pursue him by day; and if he tasted the unhallowed fruit of some Mrs. Sinclair, connubial Juno, in the softened majesty of Miss Colerain, haunted him by night.[4]

Prudence prevents him from proposing to Lady Ann, although she leads him on, and he has to fight an absurdly formal duel with Lt. Harcourt over the supposed slight on her honor. Next Sir George and Lindsay go on a tour of the north of England, and on their way back through Birmingham they visit what is evidently the Soho Works. There they see, in the exhibition room, "ornamental toys" decorated with views of the neighborhood of Southampton, which are revealed to be the work of Miss Colerain, now living quietly and industriously nearby. When Sir George calls on her, however, he finds her disconcertingly knowledgeable about his life in London, and she refuses to make any promises to him. The second volume ends effectively with their parting and their common unhappiness.

Sir George now tries the conventional cure for romantic distress, foreign travel. He and Lindsay set out for Germany, and soon find themselves at the fashionable town of Spa. Fielding, Count Colliano, and the Marquis de Valines arrive, and Sir George tries to forget his unhappiness in gambling. He soon comes to prefer the company of the convivial Fielding to that of the responsible Lindsay, and eventually he and Fielding make off to Liége with two English ladies, who had arrived at Spa with two Russian noblemen. At an inn at St. Quentin, Miss Colerain and Miss Carlill see Sir George with his partner, Mrs. Almon, but the shock of recognition does not put him back on the right path. He continues to oscillate for some time; having met Miss Colerain in the Tuilleries, he forgets her again in Paris, "the emporium of pleasure." Meeting and discussion with some French aristocrats of radical political outlook recalls him to a more responsible attitude, and he determines to work for "the amelioration of the state of mankind"; but the experienced Mrs. Almon bursts into tears, displays a "snow white leg and foot . . . in gentle agitation," and he returns to her service. He is now almost off "the road to virtue." He loses 10,000 guineas to Count Colliano, and is slighted in a coffee house by the idealistic French aristocrats because of his reputation for reckless high living. He is arrested for debt at the instigation of Count Colliano, who makes off with Mrs. Almon. Lindsay comes to Paris and discharges the debt with money raised on the estate, but has to borrow from Miss Colerain (whose finances have been restored) to pay the huge debts left by Mrs. Almon. On his release, Sir George makes for Italy, seeking revenge. On the way he calls at the château for the Marquis de Valines, only to find that the man he had been intimate with was a dismissed valet-de-chambre — so flimsy are the social values to which Sir George has descended. He hurries angrily to Turin, but fails to find Colliano. Instead, at Milan he meets another English traveler, and blasé but intelligent Honorable Mr. Bardoe, who had seen Miss Colerain in Paris and been impressed by her beauty, but had been prevented from falling in love with her by the thought of the effort that he would need to make. The third volume ends with the two men parting, in the English way, "with all the signs of polite nonchalance."[5]

In fact, however, Sir George and Bardoe become friends, and enjoy the pleasures of travelling in Italy together. Bardoe gives sensible advice to Sir George, who is still thinking of vengeance:

> "What would you have me do?"
> "Nothing," quietly answered Mr. Bardoe.

Bardoe is a perceptive and experienced man, whose apathy is partly a result of intellectual precocity and partly of an unhappy love affair. He warns Sir George, unsuccessfully, against a crafty Scots dealer, Cameron, who sells him a collection of paintings he has not even seen for £5,000.[6] They travel on toward Pescara, and near the Adriatic meet pilgrims on their way to the shrine of Our Lady of Loretto. These include a beautiful young lady in mourning, Miss Zaporo, whom the travelers assist. At this point, with the reader aware that the novel is approaching its conclusion, Bage remarks that Sir George, who has given up the idea of revenge, has made some progress toward "the temple of wisdom." At Aix-la-Chapelle, on the way back to England, he receives another lesson when he meets Fielding, now an emaciated and boastful drunkard who repudiates criticisms of his life made by "parson Paradyne" (in the spirit of Sir Moreton Everard's ridicule of James Lamounde in *James Wallace*) and serves as an object-lesson to Sir George. However, his path is still not straightforward. At Brussels he sees Lady Ann Brixworth with the imposter Marquis, disinterestedly goes to warn her, and becomes her companion. Again Miss Colerain appears, and then leaves for Ghent, whither he follows her unavailingly.

On his return to England, Sir George blames his unhappiness on Cornelia's "capricious, cruel, inexorable" temper and withdraws to rural isolation. His sister Emilia is now a widow, and Mr. Bardoe finds her attractive: together they try unsuccessfully to arouse Sir George from his melancholy. A final (and surely unnecessary) blow to Sir George occurs when he wanders into Dover, again meets Lady Ann, and then notices Miss Colerain and Miss Carlill making off in a coach. He is "seized with a very peculiar hypochondria-cism" and retires to the country, where he is looked after by an old woman and Miss Colerain's former servant, a Negro. This is the house in which Miss Colerain used to live, and he frequents her "shrubbery for exotics" and "Flora Britannica," where there is a small building with books on botany, "the poets of nature led by Thomson," including Erasmus Darwin, whose "Botanic Garden" "seemed by its use to have been the favourite of Miss Colerain," and some of her drawings. Melancholy has "marked him for her own," like the Youth in the Epitaph to Gray's "Elegy." He rouses himself, rather improbably, to question the Negro Fidel about the life of a slave, but is only really brought back to himself by finding a mysterious note in "a pretty female hand" on his table. Emilia has sought out Cornelia and brought her to him and the revelation of her love, so long concealed or doubted, leads him to kiss the ladies' hands with "no inconsiderable transport."

The novel ends with a glimpse of five years later. The usual marriages have taken place — Sir George and Cornelia, Mr. Bardoe and Emilia, Mr. Lindsay and Miss Carlill. Lady Mary is still splenetic; and Lady Ann, still unmarried, is now

...regular at St. James's church or chapel; where she has been greatly edified by the good bishop's discourses on that famous precept of St. Paul to the ladies — "If ye fall, fall not unseemly; rather fall ye with grace."

There is no account of the establishing of a "neighbourhood"; instead the final scene is of the six principals in Paris. They have gone there to see whether the French have become more serious since the Revolution:

This, I find, is partly the case; but when an English senator had said in a book, supposed to contain the collected wisdom of the nation — "That man has no rights," — the whole French people fell into a violent fit of laughter, which continues to this day. Some rights, at least, they said, might be allowed to man; the rights of suffering, and of paying taxes; these no courts would dispute. — But if, said they, men have no rights, they have wills at least; and Kings, Lords, and Priests, shall know it.

On this emphatically radical note, with the dismissive reference to Burke,[7] the novel concludes.

I   *Critical Views*

Man as He Is was quite successful in its time: a second edition
appeared in 1796, a German translation in 1798, and a third
English edition in 1819.[8] It has sometimes been considered the best
of Bage's novels. For instance, Mrs. Barbauld, on reissuing *Hermsprong* in 1810, wrote that *"Man as He Is* has more of a story, and
more variety of character."[9] She particularly praised the rendering
of Lady Paradyne, "a vain, selfish, fine lady," and of Miss Carlill,
"a quaker, in whom the author has exceedingly well hit off the
acuteness and presence of mind, and coolness in argument, by
which the society she is supposed to belong to are so much distinguished." Miss Tompkins in 1932 similarly praised the novel, suggesting that it was a remote ancestor of the novels of Thackeray.
She was impressed by the minor characters, especially the proud
returned nabob, Mr. Birimport.[10] Professor Steeves concurs in her
judgment, though noting the weaknesses of the novel in its inset
digressions and its excess of minor characters. For him there is increased subtlety in Bage's treatment of the question whether "femi-
nine purity can subsist side by side only with masculine purity."[11]
For it is left an open question whether Miss Colerain's conventionally — and genuinely — virtuous behavior did not contribute to
Sir George's perplexities and consequently to his fallings from
virtue. It is certainly notable that from the first the sensible Miss
Carlill advises Cornelia to accept Sir George rather than force him
through the probationary period most fictional lovers had to
endure. Here again Bage is questioning conventional assumptions
of the time.

The most obvious grounds for considering *Man as He Is* better
than its predecessors lie, not in the treatment of Miss Colerain, but
in the stronger narrative in which the story is embodied, and in the
credibility of Sir George. The idea of the young man of good inten-
tions becoming involved with the superficial pleasures of society
and being redeemed by the love of a good woman had no novelty
about it; perhaps its most effective earlier expression was in
Smollett's *Peregrine Pickle* (1751), the heroine of which, like Sir
George's sister, is called Emilia. The abandonment of the epistolary
method enables Bage to concentrate more on one central figure,
and contributes to the firmer movement of the plot. Even so, there
are obvious weaknesses, especially in the repetitiveness of the scenes
in which Sir George's infidelities are observed by Miss Colerain,

and in the conclusion of the love affair, which has to be brought about through the good offices of Mr. Birimport and Mr. Lindsay rather than by the lovers themselves. However, there is a satisfying sense in which the marriages at the end complete the scheme of values present throughout the novel and represent the moral victory of the rational virtues of the Lindsays and Miss Carlills over the selfish hedonism of the Fieldings and Lady Anns.

Thus Bage is successful in embodying his theme of the superiority of the "gentleman" to the "man of birth and fortune" in character and narrative. The novel, in accord with its title, is his most realistic, as he himself points out on several occasions. When describing Sir George's perplexity over his choice between Mrs. Almon and Miss Colerain, Bage breaks off to answer an imaginary objection from his lady readers:

> But be not angry with me, dear ladies: it is nature makes the enigma, not I. If the human heart is inexplicable, is it my fault? I am only a simple recorder of facts.
> Simple enough.
> What can I do? There are makers of motives enough already, more than know their trade — or I am deceived. Am I a bishop? that I should deviate from the plain path of truth and take the high priori road to ipse-dixitation? The quantity of error in the soul of this habitable globe, needs not the least increase.

Toward the end of the novel he makes the contrasting point that readers will believe in the idea of Sir George's retiring to die of love, because of its very improbability at a period when he might "cure" himself by attending taverns or hangings, by dicing, racing, and boxing, or by visiting some of the "forty thousand nuns, of the order of charity" calculated by Wendeborn[12] to be available in London: "Die! No historian, but the historian of truth, would have thought of it."

These passages, deliberately interrupting the flow of the narrative, have a mainly humorous intention, but they also draw attention to Bage's continuing interest in social attitudes and social fact. They suggest that *Man as He Is* is, like its predecessors, a novel of ideas, even if its form is more realistic. The contrasting ways of life open to Sir George are related to an overtly expressed structure of ideas, with radical attitudes like toleration and free thinking set against conservative acceptance of the *status quo.*

II *Religion and Philosophy*

The amusing remark about the "ipse dixitation" of the bishops
is related to a general account of religion and philosophy given,
lightly but clearly, in the novel. A conversation at the home of the
Anglican cleric Mr. Holford moves from literature to religion. Miss
Haubert, a wealthy and self-important lady, speaks first to Mrs.
Holford, who writes novels:

> "Very true, Mrs. Holford; I don't read many novels except yours; but I
> believe it is allowable to draw all sorts of characters as they are, and since
> it does happen that there are ingenuous [*sic*] people infidels, to be sure
> they may be drawn."
> "I wish," says Mr. Holford, "they were all drawn upon hurdles to the
> stake."
> Miss Colerain absolutely gave a little start, and was upon the point of an
> exclamation, but corrected herself, and only said, with a smile — "No,
> Mr. Holford, I must beg leave to refuse you credit on this head; your
> theory is cruel, your practice would be merciful."
> "I have no mercy for the enemies of God," answered Mr. Holford.
> "The lady," says Miss Haubert with a scornful toss of her head, "chooses
> to shew her sensibility."
> "I hope," says Miss Carlill, "if the occasion was real, thou would'st
> shew thine."

The Quaker Miss Carlill speaks up convincingly against the
authoritarian notions of Mr. Holford, who is astonished to be contradicted. When he speaks of the importance of a national religion,
she counters with a reference to the radicals' favorite example of a
free nation: " 'I pray thee,' Miss Carlill asked, 'what is the
national religion of America?' " Miss Colerain joins in with an
appeal for tolerance, which is an attitude of mind underdeveloped
by Mr. Holford but, as the conversation is presented to suggest,
highly desirable.

Bage's hostility to dogmatism affects his attitude to philosophy
as well as to religion. Miss Haubert is a professed philosopher,
although in fact she accepts any ideas that are currently fashionable. The development of her ideas is amusingly described; she
began with

> the monades and pre-established harmony of Leibnitz. This system fixed
> her faith a long time; but Malbranche came, and with him she saw all

things in God; how then should she see anything wrong? Mr. Locke shewed her clearly ideas, although begotten by outward objects, were born and brought up within; and that the mind, let it look out as sharp as it would, could hear, see, smell, taste, touch, nothing but these ideas whatever. Then says the bishop of Cloyne, how can we be certain there is anything else whatever to hear, see, smell, taste, or touch. Certain, it is more worthy of an omnipotent being, to raise ideas in the minds of intelligent creatures, by an expansion of his own — what? of his own will, than to encumber the universe with gross and senseless matter; and the phenomena were better accounted for by this sublime system, and christian faith more firmly supported. Thus, by one catholic apostolic decree, everything but spirit would have been banished for ever from the infinite regions of space, had not David Hume shewed by very clear induction from the bishop's premises, that in spite of Des Cartes — "I think, therefore I am" — it is very likely that there was no existence whatever.

This is a lively summary of the best-known ideas of Leibnitz, Malebranche,[13] Locke, Berkeley, and Hume. Miss Haubert is anxious to keep up to date, and asks Sir George if anyone has arisen to refute Hume. When he suggests Dr. Reid, she remarks, " 'Oh no — I have read him; he does not go to the bottom.' "[14] But at the end of the novel she has found a new and satisfactory comprehensive philosophy, expounded by "Robert Younge":

> This is to compose a universe, of spheres of attraction only. It is true, there is nothing to attract; but slight obstacles repel not makers of systems.

Robert Young's *An Essay on the Powers and Mechanism of Nature* appeared in 1788. Probably the confidence of Young's tone had struck Bage as inappropriate:

> By physical reasoning alone, I have found a physical principle, adequate to the purposes of explaining phenomena. A substance, actually existing, possessed of active powers, the basis of matter itself, and the agent of all effects.[15]

Bage is consistently skeptical about system-builders, and thus shows himself to be in the central tradition of Enlightenment thought, as described, for example, by Fr. Copleston:

> But the fundamental idea that human welfare depends on the exercise of reason, emancipated from the trammels of authority, of religious dogmas and of dubious metaphysical doctrine, came into prominence in the eighteenth century.[16]

So it is that when Bage gives an account of the shrine of Our Lady of Loretto and the pilgrims, he does so in a satirical tone:

> She eat and drank — that is, her sacred servants eat and drink for her — the very best of this globe's productions. Besides all this, they have covered her little cottage with a superb temple; so that she has nothing to fear from storms — except such storms as Dr. Priestley, and such magicians, are pleased sometimes to raise.

Bage follows Dr. John Moore, to whom he refers, in his skeptical attitude about the shrine (supposed to be Mary's house transferred from Nazareth by miracle) and his hostility to Roman Catholicism, seen as the unquestioning acceptance of dogma.[17] But if Bage has difficulty in extending his toleration to Roman Catholicism, it is largely because he associates it with intolerance. At all events, he can readily accept a spectrum of religious opinion from the Quakerism of Miss Carlill to the Anglicanism of Mr. Lindsay. The conversation leading up to their decision to marry one another amusingly enacts the radical idea of toleration:

> "I like not the doings of thy steeple-house," said the lady, "there is much noise and little devotion. Thy worship is mechanical."
>
> "I like very well the devotion of the friends," answered Mr. Lindsay, "as long as it is silent. When the spirit gets into the bowels, the sighs and groans of so many troubled minds, afflict me sorely. When it mounts into the tongue, so seldom proveth it to be the spirit of wisdom, that I grow sick of heavenly things."
>
> "Thou art wicked," said the lady, "if I take thee, it is out of pity to thy poor soul."
>
> "I take thee," said the gentleman, "out of pity to thy poor body."
>
> So they took one another.

There is plenty of room for variety in Bage's outlook; only the intolerant is intolerable.

III   *Discussion of Ideas*

For this reason the novel contains several lively discussions, especially of the idea of progress, which show an interest in ideas rather than a desire to reach a neat conclusion. Early in the novel, Sir George and Lindsay discuss the question of progress, and Sir George asks Lindsay when he would like to have stopped the clock:

"Is it," asked Sir George, "that you regret the elegant times of the Edwards and the Henries? Or at what period would you have stopped the progress?"

"Not at those times, certainly. Perhaps I might have chosen the beginning of the eighteenth century — before nabobs were — when wealth was more moderate, and more equal — when coxcombry, now swelled into a deluge, entered the land in a gentle current, capable of being checked in its course by the pen of the poet and the moralist — before the poor, that tolerably large proportion of the human race, forgot in all our disquisitions, political and moral, whom we despise, and to whom we owe our subsistence, and the gratification of our pride — had learned in an alehouse to imitate, at humble distance, the luxury of the tavern — before this imitation had tainted their —." Mr. Lindsay did not see that they were now under the very sign of the inn, where they had proposed to dine; his horse did; stopt, and broke the period. No matter. I hope that there is not one of my fair readers who will regret it, or pay any regard to such cold blooded, prudential declaimers.

The humorous conclusion of the scene detracts from the authority of Lindsay's argument, especially as his denunciation of the influence of the tavern coincides with his arrival at the inn. But Sir George's immediately preceding optimistic account is even more ironically placed, when he describes England as a nation "happy, strong within, terrible without, and unbounded in its resources; if you believe orthodox divines, and statemen in place." It is precisely such authorities that are discredited in the novel. Lindsay's ideal might be held conservative rather than radical — that of Smollett's Matthew Bramble in *Humphry Clinker;* hostility to the *nouveaux riches,* especially as represented by the nabobs, was a sentiment shared by moralists with diverse assumptions. The arrogance of Mr. Birimport, satirized by Bage, was typical of the type as seen by English writers from Samuel Foote in *The Nabob* (produced 1772) onward.[18] The concern about luxury and degeneration was a prominent eighteenth-century theme, especially after the publication of John Brown's *Estimate of the Life and Manners and Principles of the Times* in 1757. But, as Lois Whitney has shown, there was no clearly definable radical attitude toward it.[19] Many radicals believed simultaneously in progress and primitivism; Bage commits himself to neither.

A minor character, Mr. Mowbray, makes a judicious statement about the question: " 'We have gained in gentleness and humanity; we have lost in firmness of nerve, and strength of constitution.' " But this is not the last word. Toward the end of the novel, the theme is taken up again in the correspondence between Sir George and his sister Emilia, when she is trying to rouse him from his sentimental melancholy. Emilia is a lively and intelligent woman, like Lady Bembridge in *The Fair Syrian*. She replies effectively to her brother's denunciation of man's bestiality, rejoicing that at least he has not gone so far as to call a man a yahoo:

> I, for my part, rejoice to live in an age and country, where the animal has improved upon its nature; and attained a decent degree of cleanliness, both of body and mind. It is true, the creature knows not where to stop. What it begins with wisdom, it sometimes ends with folly. But at any rate, frippery is better than filth.

Bage gives as much authority to Emilia's moderate optimism as to Lindsay's moderate pessimism.

Similarly, a balanced attitude is implied in the reference to primitivistic ideas, which occurs when Sir George and Lindsay invite Fielding to accompany them on a journey to Germany following the course suggested by de Luc's *Letters to the Queen*.[20] Fielding's reply is amusingly in character, but its irony has some authority:

> In order to read Genesis as Genesis ought to be read, he prescribes a dozen journies into Germany; or at least the reading of them. I thank God, I can have the faith without the fatigue. Heaven forbid I should deny that the minors [sic] of Hartz are the happiest of human beings. How should they be otherwise, when they see their wives but once a week? It is true, their bread might be better, and they might be allowed onions at least to eat with it. But after all, they are made ample amends by their wives scrubbing brushes on Saturday night, and by going with clean faces to church on Sunday.
>
> Heaven forbid too, that I should deny the happiness of that other class of felicitants, who live in the pure stile of simple nature, "When man and beast, joint tenants of the shade," performed their functions so lovingly together, that nothing, quite like it, is to be seen in all London.

Although Fielding is an unsympathetic character, his view is that of common sense. Bage finds extravagance of any kind, including that of the primitivists, amusing, so long as it does not concern matters of vital principle. Even when he is at his most serious, Bage does not force human nature into a convenient shape to suit his thesis. At one point in the novel the rational Lindsay tries to dissuade Sir George from issuing a challenge to a duel in defense of Miss Colerain's honor. Sir George brushes aside Lindsay's reasoned case:

"To strong feelings, arguments will always be opposed in vain."

"And yet, my dear Sir George, arguments have been often applied to change the feelings of mankind; have succeeded sometimes, and man has been the better for it . . . : this might be the case here."

But Sir George is stubbornly determined:

"I can only exhibit to your wondering eyes, the triumph of feeling, over reason."

"Alas!" says Lindsay, "you are not solitary in this."

Later Fielding challenges Lindsay to a duel, and the philosopher finds that he cannot refuse (although the events of the plot prevent the duel from taking place). Bage shares the radical conviction of the Enlightenment that the application of reason to human affairs is the key to progress, but he is well aware also of the recalcitrance of human nature. For this reason, his novels are not simply didactic but display a variety of attitudes and ideas.

IV *Criticism of Society*

Nevertheless it is clear that there are some forms of human behavior, and these mostly associated with the upper classes, which are totally unacceptable to Bage. One of these is the duel, which is treated in this novel, as in earlier ones, in a spirit of amused contempt. For instance, nothing could be more absurd than Mowbray's fighting a duel over his wife's nonexistent honor, unless it were Lt. Harcourt's attempt to defend Lady Ann's. Sir George's duel with him is absurdly formal but satisfies the rules:

Thus the lady was avenged; honour was satisfied; and nothing remained to be done by the combatants, but to pay the proper compliments on each other's valour.

Later, Harcourt apologizes for his conduct, having discovered that the whole affair was a result of the schemings of Lady Ann. Bage's other comment on dueling is direct, in the form of a compliment to

. . . a gentleman of some quality in the republic of letters, who has lately done us, the humble novelists of Great Britain, the honour to put himself at our head. He has taught us that the duel is the grand support of good manners, and that a score or so of lives annually, is a cheap purchase of this precious commodity. I am convinced.

As so often Bage uses an effective irony to convey his criticism of a practice of which he disapproves.

Bage's radical hostility to various aspects of upper-class behavior finds expression also in the amusing scene in which the Reverend Mr. Holfod goes to offer Miss Colerain some advice, having heard rumors of her having an affair with Sir George. The contrast between his wordliness and her simplicity is well sustained:

"And the report is, madam, that you have entered into terms with him."
"Terms, sir!" said Miss Colerain.
"Not, madam," continued the parson, "that I have anything to say, particularly, against Sir George Paradyne; nor am I so ignorant of the world as not to know that gentlemen do form such connections very often; neither am I so illiberal as to suppose, that if such connections be honourably adhered to, according to the terms, that it is unpardonable in the sight of God."
"No, Sir?" said Miss Colerain, with astonished simplicity.
"No, madam; Mr. Madan has corrected some false ideas on his head, and proved, that what God allowed to the Patriarchs, though now wrong, cannot be eternally reprobated by his justice and mercy."

The Reverend Martin Madan's well-meant advocacy of polygamy rather than prostitution for "surplus" females in *Thelyphthora* in 1780 was widely criticized and satirized.[21] Bage is not shocked or indignant but amused by the proposal, and he associates it neatly with laxity of moral standards in the upper classes and with clerical sycophancy. Mr. Holford goes on to offer Miss Colerain his "friendship and good services":

"To what purpose, Sir?"
"I am not, madam, a rigid censor of the private failings of human nature; neither am I insensible to the charms of beauty, but I think always, the utmost external decency and decorum ought to be preserved, for the sake of good example to the lower classes — and —"
"This," said Miss Colerain, rising from her seat, "this, from a clergyman, and married! — you have still ideas that ought to be corrected; assuredly, I am not the person you have done me the honour to suppose I am; nor will I make terms with Sir George Paradyne, even for the friendship and consolations of the reverend Mr. Holford, to whom I have the honour of wishing a good morning." On saying this, Miss Colerain left the room.

There is no doubt about Bage's moral position; he amusingly condemns upper-class behavior, and the hypocrisies and pretenses involved in providing a suitable "example to the lower classes."

When public issues become prominent in the novel, Bage's attitude toward them is always that of the radicals. For example, the brief interpolated story of the Negro slave Fidel expresses disgust with the treatment of slaves and sympathy for their sufferings. Fidel was born in Africa, sold for "a Birmingham musket" by his father when he was twelve, and taken to Jamaica. He served a good master well, but was ill-treated by his brutal son, until rescued by Miss Colerain's father. The son desired the Negro girl whom Fidel loved, and when she refused him, first raped her himself and then encouraged his steward to rape, and then whip, her. The wretched girl drowned herself. Fidel killed the steward and was put on trial, but acquitted, and brought back to England by Mr. Colerain. This horrifying story is far too strong for its place in the novel, and Sir George's bequest of £50 per annum to Fidel seems a hardly adequate response. Yet the inclusion of the story shows Bage's sympathy with the Quakers and other radicals who were making vigorous efforts to have the slave trade abolished.[22]

V   *Political Commitment*

The changed political atmosphere of England in the years immediately following the French Revolution, the more open and vigorous conflict between radical and conservative ideas, is reflected in the greater amount of political reference in *Man as He Is* compared with *James Wallace.* Lord Auschamp is disappointed in Sir George as a political ally:

> He never could make him comprehend that great political truth, that power is always right; and the consequent necessity of supporting government in all its motions.

The courtier's politics are neatly summarized. Auschamp's views are the opposite of those of Lindsay, as becomes obvious when they are discussing the latter's attitudes as a possible tutor for Sir George:

> "Betwixt the morals that befit a gentleman, and that which is calculated for common life, I make no doubt you distinguish properly."
> "I presume your Lordship means manners, not morals."
> "Mr. Lindsay, I understand the English language tolerably well. —

There is no necessity to suppose I mean anything but what I say."

"I beg your Lordship's pardon. There may be a commodious morality for the exclusive use of the rich and great; but I own myself unacquainted with it."

It is consistent that when Auschamp asks Lindsay to make sure that Sir George shall have an adequate sense of the superiority of England over other countries, they agree on that assumption but disagree over the reasons for it. The conservative Auschamp attributes it to "the indulgent family on the throne," the radical Lindsay to the rule of law.

The political discussion which Sir George has in Paris with such French radical aristocrats as Lafayette and Lally-Tolendal[23] (for here as in other places in the novel Bage introduces well-known figures from contemporary life) gives him the opportunity to stress the better side of the British constitution:

"Your nation, Chevalier," said the Count, "stands the foremost upon the globe, for liberty and good government. What, according to you, are the essential principles?"

"I believe," Sir George answered, "the grand secret lies in making your own laws, and granting our own money. You impose this trouble on your monarch. I advise you to take that fatiguing part of his business off his hands. Not that we do not make bad laws sometimes, and give money for foolish purposes; but however we may cut our fingers, we take care of our throats."

Later, when his sister tries to persuade him to shake off his melancholy and go into Parliament, Sir George is scornful:

No, Emilia, never will I be member of a body, pretending to the suffrages of a nation, and constituted by so diminutive a part of it — who give to a minister all he asks — who trust him confidently where he ought least to be trusted — in the business of destroying mankind.

In part this is a mere excuse, but the criticism which it expresses is authoritative. The franchise is too restricted; the House too subservient. If Bage is aware of the worth, from the radical point of view, of the British constitution, with its limitations on the power of the monarchy, he is also aware of how ineffectual Parliament could be for expressing the viewpoint of any but a small class. Thus a minor character, Mr. Mowbray, expresses a belief in the value of political parties:

> The keen eye of opposition is alone competent to see the barbed hook, which too often lies concealed under the splendid baits of government.

Characteristically, Bage does not advocate any theoretical panacea such as the withering away of the state: his radicalism takes the practical form of upholding a system which gives a chance to those affected by ministerial decisions to scrutinize and object.

The most explicit political passages, however, are those — like the final paragraph of the novel — which are directed against the political philosophy of conservatism as expressed by Edmund Burke. It is well known how the publication of Burke's *Reflections on the Revolution in France* in 1790 stirred many prominent Radicals to answer, including Paine in *The Rights of Man* and Mackintosh in his *Vindiciae Gallicae.*[24] Bage makes his indignant reply to Burke in this novel, and not only on its last page. The satire on Lord Auschamp's place-seeking conformity, and the praise of free institutions and the rule of law in the conversation with the French aristocrats, point in the same direction. But it is in relation to Miss Zaporo that the argument becomes most emphatic and cogent. She follows the rigid Roman Catholic conservatism of her mother, rather than the libertarianism of her father, who took part in the Transylvanian rising. She ascribes the rising to the influence of "certain books" from Holland, France, and England which suggested that government was instituted "solely for the good of the people," and to the planned abolition by the Emperor of the privileges of the nobility, including feudal tenures. Miss Zaporo believes that the extension of liberty would have been disastrous:

> "That respectable series of veneration from the vassal to the monarch," replied Miss Zaporo, "would then have been lost. We should have seen no more of that generous loyalty to rank."

Bage then breaks into the novel in his own person to comment on the similarity between Miss Zaporo's views and those of Burke:

> These enlarged and liberal sentiments of Miss Zaporo's, have always struck me as being the true foundation of most of the existing governments of this our globe. A book which has lately enchanted all kings, all queens,

all bishops — save one — all good old women, and half an university, has been wrote to amplify, and to sublime them.[25]

Bage ironically praises the eloquence of Burke's writing, particularly "the apotheosis of the lovely queen into a star" and the lamentation over the passing of chivalric loyalties, culminating in the sentence, "I thought ten thousand swords must have leaped from their scabbards, to avenge even a look that threatened her with insult!"[26]

I was quoting this with a generous enthusiasm to an old friend who lives a very retired life, and troubles himself but little about the politics of this world. The muslces of his face contracted into a sort of grin — "Ten thousand pens," said he, "must start from their ink-stands, to punish the man who dares attempt to restore the empire of prejudice and passion. The age of chivalry, heaven be praised, is gone. The age of truth and reason has commenced, and will advance to maturity in spite of cants or bishops. Law, — active, invincible, avenging law, is here the knight-errant that redresses wrongs, protects damsels, and punishes the base miscreants who oppress them." ... Philosophy and commerce have transformed that *generous loyalty to rank,* into attachment to peace, to law, to the general happiness of mankind; that *proud submission* and *dignified obedience,* into an unassuming consciousness of natural equality; and that *subordination of the heart* into an honest veneration of superior talents, conjoined with superior benevolence.
I did not invite my friend to dinner.

Bage's hostility to Burke's view is so strong, it would seem, that he is prepared to abandon his narrative in order to insert this reply. All the radical values underlying his criticism of upper-class society are made explicit here: "an unassuming consciousness of natural equality," in particular, is a striking antithesis to the Burkean belief in "proud submission" and "dignified obedience." The "man of birth and fortune" is to give way to the truly able, truly public-spirited man, in a system of law.

It is in key with these radical sentiments, and in a tone characteristic of Bage, that at the end of the novel the possibility that Sir George may one day inherit the title of Earl of Auschamp should be described as

a most agreeable metamorphosis; and likely to be relished in England, when titles shall be nick-names only, in the rest of Europe.

Here Bage is very close in attitude to Paine.[27] He is able to extract some amusement from the idea of English traditionalism, but he believes in the new England of the "upright commercians" to whom titles would be absurdities. Thus it is fitting that some of the most enthusiastic pages of the novel should be those concerned with Birmingham and the Soho Works:

> A Scene of a far different kind was preparing for Sir George at Birmingham, a place scarcely more distinguished for useful and ornamental manufacture, than for gentlemen who excel in natural philosophy, in mechanics, and in chemistry. One of these has a manufactory at a small distance from the town, scarce better known in England, than in France and Italy, Holland, Germany and Russia, or wherever commerce has displayed the British flag.

Bage is not exaggerating. R. E. Schofield has noted:

> The Soho works early became a place to be visited, one of the wonders of "modern" England that all travellers wished to see.[28]

Bage makes it sound as if Miss Colerain almost became the only female member of the Lunar Society, when the proprietor of the factory says to Sir George:

> She shuns acquaintance. She has indeed honoured my table with her company twice; when I have been favoured with the company of Dr. Priestley; with that of Mr. Keir, the well-known translator and elucidator of Macquer's Chemistry; or the celebrated author of the botanic garden, to whom all arts and all sciences have obligation. But without some such inducement, she never stirs abroad.[29]

In this passage, Bage makes clear his own commitment to the new England of Priestley rather than the old England of Burke. If the antithesis he states to "the man of birth and fortune" is simply "the gentleman," and if he reverts in *Man as He Is* to a titled hero, these are elements of convention which he does not have the originality or consistency to avoid. But the central emphasis of the novel, both in its hostilities and in its endorsements, is undeniable. As the situation in England following the French Revolution caused a sharpening of political controversy, Bage made clearer than ever his own radical views.

CHAPTER 7

Hermsprong:
Satire and Social Criticism

BAGE'S last and best-known novel, *Hermsprong: or, Man as He Is Not,*was published at the Minerva Press in 1796. On this occasion Bage employs a narrator for the story, one Gregory Glen, who begins with great vivacity in offering an explanation of his motives for writing:

Not for fame, certainly: No, not for fame; not to instruct the good people of England; for wisdom is there in its greatest perfection; nor is it my intention to make my readers laugh, — for these are serious times; nor weep, — for I must first weep myself, as Horace says, and Melpomene is not my favourite muse; in short, I am not determined to write by any of the reasons which authors usually chuse to assign. My motive is of tolerable universality notwithstanding. Not that I want money neither; but I see those who do, — beggars of princely denomination — on thrones — on wooden legs.[1]

Glen follows this with a lively and amusing account of his own life, before describing the events which make up the story.

Bage's narrator is one of the strengths of the novel. Wayne Booth in *The Rhetoric of Fiction* in 1961 placed Bage with the Diderot of *Jacques le fataliste* in having discovered new uses for a type of narrator derived from Sterne:

In general the successful imitations have been based on a discovery of new uses for this kind of narrator. Diderot and Bage, for example, both succeeded with genuinely new works.... Bage, in *Hermsprong* (1796), embodied his satirical message, somewhat in the manner of Swift, in his narrator's imperfections.[2]

That Sterne is in the background is evident from such passages as the conclusion of the third chapter, where Glen archly reports a conversation between himself and a "critic":

There is a person — *vel hic vel haec* — no matter, — who does me the favour to marshall my commas and colons, — regulate my ifs and ands, — and correct my errors of orthography, who at this place surprised, and indeed vexed me, by a bolder criticism. So far, says my critic, you have amused yourself drawing characters; if that be the end and intention of your book, I have nothing more to say than to advise you to study brevity and Theophrastus. If your design be, as I understand it, to exhibit actions and events, I submit it to your superior judgment, if it might not be altogether as agreeable to your readers, to form for themselves the characters of your drama, from their good or evil deeds. Tell us what they do, and we shall be able to find out whether they were wise or foolish, rough or smooth, discreet or vain, or drunk or sober. To which I replied, — but whether by a kiss or a cuff, I am not at present disposed to say.

This is neat but derivative; the playfulness is in the manner of Sterne. The tone which Booth has in mind comes over as something fresh in, for example, Glen's account of his vacillations about leaving London for the country:

It was, however, no unfavourable circumstance, that as my purse declined, I began to call the amusements of London frivolous, and when it was exhausted, I said they were contemptible. *O rus! quando te ego aspiciam?* was oft upon my lips; and I read Thomson's Seasons by way of corroborant. Yet, though I sighed for the country, and detested, or said I detested the town, it was not without some violence that I prevailed upon my legs to carry me over Westminster-Bridge, one fine morning in May. As I advanced I congratulated myself on my escape; looked back, and sighed; saw St. Paul's towering with majestic grandeur; became sensible I had not sufficiently examined that superb edifice; walked one hundred yards towards it; felt in my pockets; called the town a sink of iniquity; turned again and trod, with angry strides, the road to Exeter.

The self-satisfaction of the conventional moralist is avoided by this comic treatment. The reader is most conscious of the narrator in the early chapters, before the narrative develops its own interest, so that Booth's claim goes beyond the evidence. But it is the ironical tone of Gregory Glen which creates the initial atmosphere of the book and constitutes an important part of its success.

The scene of most of the novel is the "small, clean village of

Grondale" in Cornwall, dominated by the gouty authoritarian
Lord Grondale, whose main supporter is the rector, Dr. Blick, "a
man perfectly orthodox in matters of church and state, such as
these bad times require." Lord Grondale has one daughter, the
beautiful and benevolent Caroline Campinet, and the action begins
with the bolting of her horse on Lippen Crag. She is saved from
hurtling over the cliff only by the timely arrival of an heroic stranger, who claims to have learned his manner of life from "the sons
of nature" and, on the arrival of Lord Grondale, gives grave
offense by his lack of deference to rank.

Meanwhile, Caroline Campinet's closest friend, the heiress
Maria Fluart, is at her guardian's in Falmouth. Mr. Sumelin is an
"opulent and respectable" banker, an unusual man, who doubts
whether monarchs are divinely appointed; his wife and elder
daughter, Harriet, are, however, perfectly conventional, a situation
which gives rise to effective social comedy. Miss Fluart and Miss
Campinet are contrasted in character (like so many comparable
pairs, from Clarissa Harlowe and Anna Howe to Jane and Elizabeth Bennet, and including Julia Foston and Laura Stanley). Miss
Fluart is as vivacious and unconventional as Miss Campinet is
earnest and dutiful. Miss Fluart writes to tell her friend about the
elopement of Harriet with her father's clerk, Mr. Fillygrove, and
her restoration to the family by a gentleman with the "monstrous
Germanish" name of Hermsprong, who is an American by birth
but has lately been in France. No novel-reader would doubt that he
is to be disclosed also as Miss Campinet's heroic rescuer.

Later, Miss Fluart comes to stay at Grondale Hall, and encourages Miss Campinet to resist her father's tyranny; she even flirts
with Lord Grondale to ease her friend's situation. The two young
ladies return together to Falmouth, where a new suitor for Miss
Campinet arrives in Sir Phillip Chestrum, a wealthy and insipid
young gentleman who presents an unfavorable contrast in every
way to Hermsprong. A match between Miss Campinet and Sir
Phillip is approved by the parents, Lord Grondale hoping that it
will put an end to his daughter's aberrant feeling for Hermsprong.
In fact, however, he is progressing in her affections in Falmouth by
his rationality in conversation and his beneficence in action.

Lord Grondale invites Sir Phillip to Grondale Hall and tries to
force his daughter to marry him. He also asks Miss Fluart to leave
before the ceremony, and a weeping figure dashes from the house.
When the wedding is about to take place, however, the "bride"

reveals herself as Miss Fluart. Lord Grondale attempts to prevent her from leaving, but she produces a pistol and makes an intrepid exit. By now, Lord Grondale has engaged his lawyer to make a case against Hermsprong on the grounds of subversive activities, such as reading Paine's *Rights of Man* and criticizing the British constitution. But when he is brought to court, Hermsprong reveals that he is Sir Charles Campinet, son of Lord Grondale's elder brother and rightful heir to the title and estates. Lord Grondale retires, discomfited. The impending happy ending is held up by the return of the dutiful Miss Campinet to her stricken father, an act condemned by Hermsprong as irrational. He plans to return to America and establish a community there with the friends he has made in England:

I have sixty thousand acres of uncleared land upon the Potowmac. It cost me little. I have imagined a society of friends within a two mile ring; and I have imagined a mode of making it happy. In this, it is possible, I may not reach the point I desire; but with common prudence, we cannot fail of plenty, and in time of affluence.

Miss Fluart alone remains skeptical about this scheme, so appealing to idealists of the period (notably Coleridge and Southey, with their unfulfilled scheme of Pantisocracy). She will not come without her friend Miss Campinet, and expresses herself with characteristic vivacity: ''...if she is not amongst your collection, you may grub wood by yourselves.'' In fact emigration proves unnecessary. Hermsprong and Caroline exchange explanatory letters; Lord Grondale suffers a timely stroke and expires in a spirit of forgiveness. The ''society of friends'' which Hermsprong had planned on the Potomac is established in Cornwall, and Gregory Glen, the intermittent narrator, closes his improbable story with the inevitable wedding.

I *Tone and Irony*

The plot is conventional and not important; the superiority of *Hermsprong* over Bage's earlier novels lies in its compression and its sustained ironical tone. As the subtitle, *Man as He Is Not,* suggests, Bage is deliberately offering a perfect hero, the most consciously noble of savages; he is not attempting realism, but making use of a literary device which had pervaded much eighteenth-century writing critical of "civilisation," as can be seen from H. N. Fairchild's study *The Noble Savage*.[3] Nevertheless, it had not provided the hero of an English novel since Mrs. Aphra Behn's romance *Oroonoko* in 1698. In this, its relevant predecessor is Voltaire's *L'Ingénu*. Voltaire's fable was translated and known in England,[4] and furnished some of the material used by Bage. In *L'Ingénu* (which is cautiously set by Voltaire in 1689 and attributed to one Father Quesnel), the Abbot of Kerkabon and his sister meet a young "Indian," who has come from England and wishes to learn about France. His character is open and determined, as his reply to a question about his name suggests:

"I have always been called the Frank-one," answered the Huron, "and they have fixed this name on me in England because I always say freely what I think, as I always do what I please."

The Huron turns out to be the Abbot's nephew, who had gone with his family to America as a child. He falls in love with the beautiful Miss St. Ives, whose beauty "converts" him to Catholicism. He learns about France by experience. He is shut up in the Bastille with a Jansenist, and makes rapid intellectual progress through reading and discussion:

The reason of his displaying so much genius was as much owing to his savage education, as to the strength of his understanding; for not having learned any thing in his infancy, he had not imbibed any prejudices; his mind, not being warped by error, had remained in its original purity.

He converts the Jansenist to a form of Deism. Meanwhile, the Abbot and Miss St. Ives have been trying to obtain his release. The virtuous Abbot is quite unsuccessful, while Miss St. Ives has to give herself to the powerful St. Pouange in order to achieve her end. She falls ill with remorse, and despite the Huron's profession of continuing love for her, she dies. St. Pouange feels remorse, and helps the Huron later to achieve promotion in the army. The ex-Jansenist obtains a benefice, and takes as his motto, "Misfortunes are good for something." The fable thus combines wit and indignation in Voltaire's best manner. Its brevity precludes development or variety of character, but the condemnation of a corrupt and authoritarian society is lucid and assured.

The parallels between Hermsprong and the Huron are obvious.

Both are Europeans, brought up among Red Indians and thus escaping the prejudices of civilization. Hermsprong describes the results of his upbringing thus:

I cannot learn to surrender my opinion from complaisance, or from any principle of adulation. Nor can I learn to suppress the sentiments of a free-born mind, from any fear, religious or political. Such uncourtly obduracy has my savage education produced.

Both the Huron and Hermsprong are used to show up the empty pretensions of European civilization, although the events of Voltaire's story are more extravagant and simplified. The noble savage of Bage is closer to Voltaire than to Rousseau, because of the predominantly ironical tone of the writing. Voltaire is also more important for *Hermsprong* than Smollett's *Sir Launcelot Greaves,* which provided the plot with the incident of the runaway horse and the courageous hero.[5]

There is one Oriental anecdote, too, in *Hermsprong* which is immediately suggestive of Voltaire. Mr. Sumelin announces some startling news at the breakfast table to his unimaginative wife and daughter:

"There is very extraordinary news from Constantinople, my dear," said the banker; "fifty of the Grand Signior's wives were brought to bed in one night."

"Fifty!, Mr. Sumelin," said the astonished lady.

"Fifty," replied the banker.

"Wives, papa?" asked Miss Sumelin.

"No — not precisely what we should call wives in England, but something very like them. You must know, the Grand Signior buys his ladies; and, for the honour of your sex, I must tell you, that some of them have cost him £1000 English money; whilst a man who sells for £100 must be extraordinary."

The main point of the anecdote lies not, however, in its evidence of the "honour" of women, but in the argument that follows the births. The Grand Signior is very angry, and has the chief seraglio guard beheaded. Eventually, however, the Mufti calms him, in a long oration, which Mr. Sumelin summarizes:

"The purport of it, was to shew, that the power of the prophet of God was not limited to so small exertions. If God pleased, all the women in the world might be brought to bed in one night; and perhaps the prophet might intend to reward the piety of our most august monarch, king of kings of the earth, by this display of his unbounded liberality. What do you think of it, my dear?''

"To be sure, Mr. Sumelin, if it be true, it's rather odd."

The anecdote, like many of Voltaire's, is directed against the credulity of unthinking believers; the comedy is increased by having Mrs. Sumelin as its auditor.

II *Criticism of Society*

In *Hermsprong,* Bage's radical ideas find their expression in a variety of ways, including discussion and satire. The treatment of religion shows this. At one point Hermsprong describes the attempt of his devout mother to convert the Indian Chief Lontac. She calculates that "greater sins than hers might be expiated, by a conversion to Christianity of a few Nawdoessie females."[6] After she has told him the Christian stories about the creation of the world, Lontac recounts some of his tribal stories. These she immediately dismisses:

"But this is so excessively absurd," said my mother.

"I have not called your wonders absurd," Lontac replied; "I thought it more decent to believe."

"What have I told you so preposterous?" asked my mother.

"Many things far removed from the course of nature," Lontac replied; "I do not presume to call them preposterous. It is better to believe than contradict."

A form of this anecdote had been used by earlier antidogmatic writers, including Benjamin Franklin.[7] The bland deistic eclecticism of the chief is lightly and pointedly elevated above the arrogance of orthodoxy.

In the treatment of Dr. Blick, the radicalism of Bage finds its expression in satire. For instance, Dr. Blick preaches a vigorous sermon on the subject of the Birmingham riots of 1791; but his view of these events is clearly distinguished from the narrator's own:

It was the 14th of July, an anniversary of the riots at Birmingham; where a quantity of pious makers of buttons, inspired by our holy mother, had pulled down the dissenting meeting houses, together with the dwelling houses of the most distinguished of that unpopular sect. The Reverend Dr. Blick did not say this was exactly right; he only said, that liberty had grown into licentiousness, and almost into rebellion.

Considering the closeness of these events to him, Bage's tone is remarkably detached and ironic. The sermon itself is a sonorous and amusing parody of the conversative rhetoric whose master was Burke:

"If ever the Church can be in danger, it is so now," said the good Doctor. "Now, when the atheistical lawgivers of a neighbouring country, have laid their sacrilegious hands upon the sacred property of the church; now, when the whole body of dissenters here have dared to imagine the same thing. These people, to manifest their gratitude for the indulgent, too indulgent toleration shewn them, have been filling the nation with inflammatory complaints against a constitution, the best the world ever saw, or will ever see; against a government, the wisest, mildest, freest from corruption, that the purest page of history has ever yet exhibited."

The peroration is a fine expression of Dr. Blick's perfect orthodoxy:

"But," said the Doctor, rising in energy, "what can be expected from men who countenance the abominable doctrines of the rights of man? Rights contradicted by nature, which has given us an ascending series of inequality, corporeal and mental; and plainly pointed out the way to those political distinctions created by birth and rank. To this failure of respect to the dignitaries of the nation, and, let me add, to the dignitaries of the church, is to be ascribed the alarming evils which threaten the overthrow of all religion, all government, all that is just and equitable upon earth."

With such sentiments had Dr. Horsley brought the members of the House of Lords to their feet at the climax of a famous sermon in 1793.[8] Like Miss Zaporo's denunciation of liberal ideas in *Man as He Is,* the sermon (which is better integrated into the novel) represents the outlook to which Bage is totally opposed.

Dr. Blick is being criticized for his political rather than his religious position. His relation to his patron Lord Grondale represents the subservience of the Church of England to the ruling class which radicals consistently deplored. His sycophancy is emphasized. On one occasion Lord Grondale's housekeeper, Mrs. Stone, who is hoping to marry his Lordship in return for her various services to him, turns the conversation to marriage. Lord Grondale, however,

neatly defends himself by referring to the Reverend Martin
Madan's suggestion of consuetudinage (accepted also by the Reverend Mr. Holford in *Man as He Is,* to Miss Coleraine's horror).[9]
Lord Grondale becomes indignant when Mrs. Stone claims that a
woman risks losing heaven by giving herself to a man outside
marriage:

"The cant of methodists!" said his Lordship. "The church of England
has more liberal notions; — has she not, Doctor?"

In his appeals to Dr. Blick, Lord Grondale was seldom disappointed;
nor had he now reason to complain, except of prolixity; for the learned
divine, having, at great length, explained how marriage and consuetudinage existed together in patriarchal times, proved that what was right
then could not be wrong now; and that it was scarce possible a Lord
should be wrong at any time.

An even more pointed exchange occurs when the exasperated Lord
Grondale is considering disinheriting his daughter for her disobe-
dience:

"I will leave my fortune to hospitals," continued his Lordship, "or to
Bedlam."

"Your Lordship need not be reduced to that extremity," said the Doctor; "there are worthy individuals still, though the age is corrupt; men who
would use your Lordship's bounty for the service of mankind — men
who —"

"Are dressed in black," said his Lordship, "and, merely to serve mankind, pant after mitres and lawn sleeves."

Dr. Blick deserves the sarcasm, and Lord Grondale has reached a
point of exasperation at which even sycophancy is inadequate.

Dr. Blick's outlook is based on his social subservience, and is
buttressed by a scheme of religious values in which charity is held to
be less important than faith. This is shown in a conversation
between Dr. Blick and Miss Campinet about the active benevolence
of Hermsprong to the villagers of Grondale who have been stricken
by a storm:

"But, Madam, he is a proud haughty young man, who thinks too well
of himself to pay a proper respect to his betters. Over and above this,
Madam, he is an infidel; and you know, without faith our best works are
splendid sins."

"So this profusion of benevolence is with you, Doctor, only a splendid sin?"

"Nothing more, Miss Campinet. A pure stream cannot flow from a corrupt fountain."

"You prefer faith, then, to charity?"

"Certainly Miss Campinet, — to everything: so, I hope, do you?"

"I hope I believe as I ought; but I own, Doctor, I feel a bias in favour of such splendid sins."

The humanistic emphasis on charity and socially useful activity is characteristic of Bage. The curate Woodcock, who sympathizes with and helps the poor of the parish when Dr. Blick offers only advice, is an example of the best in the Christian tradition. But Bage has also made the radical suggestion that Christianity is not the necessary source of a sound morality in his account of the Indians and of Hermsprong himself.

The treatment of Dr. Blick is typical of the way in which *Hermsprong* makes its social criticism; upper-class manners and morals are subjected to effective satire, the tone of which is predominantly genial. Lord Grondale's treatment of Mrs. Stone is to be expected of a man whose life has been devoted to the selfish pursuit of pleasure. His grounds contain a pavilion, an octagonal pleasure-house adorned with paintings of Imogen, Atalanta, and Venus. But whereas in *Mount Henneth* Annabella had been in real danger from Lord Winterbottom, in *Hermspring* Miss Fluart is well able to cope with Lord Grondale's elderly advances:

"Upon my word, my dear Miss Fluart," said his Lordship, getting down after her as fast as he was able, "you are quite a prude today. I thought you superior to the nonsense of your sex, the making such a rout about a kiss."

"A kiss! Lord bless me," said Miss Fluart, "I thought, from the company your Lordship had brought me into, and the mode of your attack, you had wanted to undress me."

Lord Grondale burst into an immoderate laugh, and declared it was the drollest idea in the world.

The humor of the scene does not preclude the condemnation of Lord Grondale's way of life, which is more explicit in the somber account of his annual house-party for gambling.

The radical preference for simplicity and hostility to sophistication pervades the novel, but is explicit, for example, in the contrast between Hermsprong himself and the buck, as wittily described by Miss Fluart to her friend:

> Did you ever see a buck, Caroline? Not the tame creature of the park or the forest, but the wild buck of London or Paris; an animal which bounds over all fences; breakfasts in London; dines at Newmarket; devotes six days and nights to the fields of sport, of hazard, and champagne; and having done all that he has to do, that is, lost his money, returns to town, to the arms of his fair Rosabella; dozes away forty-eight hours between love and compunction; awakes, damns all impertinent recollections; sends for an Israelite, signs, and is again a buck.

Against this extravagance and selfishness must be set the simplicity and beneficence of the hero, with his habits of drinking water and traveling on foot. When, in conversation with Hermsprong, Dr. Blick learns of his walking, he is astonished:

> "You have travelled then, I presume, Sir; but you are too young to have travelled much."
> "Too young, perhaps, to have travelled to much purpose; but I have trod much ground."
> "Trod, Sir! — Is that term proper? I presume you did not travel on foot."
> "Chiefly so, Sir."
> "On foot, Sir?"
> "On foot."
> This was a circumstance that could not fail, in a mind like Dr. Blick's, to abate something of the respect which the gentleman's dress and manner might have produced.

Only those who had to traveled on foot in late eighteenth-century England. For the rich to do so was an unpardonable eccentricity, as a foreign observer, C. P. Moritz, noted in 1782:

> A traveller on foot in this country seems to be considered as a sort of wild man, or an out-of-the-way being, who is stared at, pitied, suspected, and shunned by everybody that meets him.[10]

Hermsprong's behavior exhibits a consistent tendency to reduce the differences between the social classes and is consequently incomprehensible to the supporters of the *status quo*.

These may be found not only in the upper class but also among the bourgeoisie. Mrs. Sumelin is perfectly conventional and restricted in her outlook. Her reaction to the news of her favorite daughter's elopement with a mere clerk is therefore comically different from that of her phlegmatic and unconventional husband:

"Well, and for what is all this noise and pother, Mrs. Sumelin? Your daughter is gone to be married, that's all. I suppose you intended she should marry one day?"

"But to marry so much beneath her, Mr. Sumelin, — and such a coxcomb."

"As to his being a coxcomb, my dear, we must set that down as a circumstance in Harriet's favour; coxcombry being the most approved qualification of man, in the mind of woman; and as to his being beneath her, I know not what that means."

"No! Mr. Sumelin: So rich as you are, and a young lady with your daughter's accomplishments."

"As to riches, Mrs. Sumelin, they are my own, and at my own disposal. I may give Mrs. Fillygrove a large fortune, and I may not. It is true, I do not much like masses of money in the hands of fools; but she is my daughter; I shall not let her want; and her puppy husband may one day be weaned of his folly, and make as respectable a man as his poverty of understanding will permit."

This is an admirable comic scene which has accurately been said by Dorothy Blakey to foreshadow the relationship of the Bennets in *Pride and Prejudice*.[11] In it is amusingly enacted a serious contrast of social attitudes.

III   *Feminism and the Politics of Moderation*

It is wholly consistent that when Hermsprong dines with the Sumelins his radical ideas strike Mrs. Sumelin as ridiculous. The conversation turns at one point to women's education and capacities. Mary Wollstonecraft's *A Vindication of the Rights of Woman* had been published in 1792, so that the case for feminism was known at the time, although it was not consistently emphasized in radical circles. Mr. Sumelin, a good conversationalist, draws Hermsprong out on the subject, arguing against his view that English women have too little liberty:

"Perhaps," Mr. Hermsprong returned, "we may be reconciled, if, as I suspect, you mean that English young ladies of a certain age and rank have too much liberty of person. This I am ready to grant you, *pro gratia;* if you will have the goodness to allow they have too little liberty of mind."

"To so courteous an antagonist," said Sumelin, "I would allow all I could; but this — this is really too much. And, pray, Sir, when they carry their pretty persons to routs and Ranelaghs, balls and masquerades, do they not carry their minds with them?"

"Yes," Mr. Hermsprong answered, — "such as they have, minds imprisoned, — which instead of ranging the world of physics and metaphysics, are confined to the ideas of these routs and Ranelaghs, with their adjuncts of dress, cards and scan — I beg pardon — I mean criticism."

Hermsprong refers with approval to Mary Wollstonecraft's view that women's mode of education "turns the energies of their minds on trifles," and argues that "parents, in their modes of education, must make less distinction of sex." This argument is dismissed by Mr. Sumelin as "pretty and sentimental," but abstract and unrealistic. The scene ends with Hermsprong's withdrawal and comments upon him by the worldly Mrs. Sumelin and her daughter, and the guests:

"His notions are quite shocking," said Mrs. Sumelin; "don't you think so, Miss Campinet?"

"I thought his ideas singular, madam," this young lady answered, "but not shocking."

"But they are vastly foolish," said Miss Sumelin; "how absurd it was to talk of women doing men's work!"

"One may excuse the absurdity, supposing it to be one," said Miss Campinet, "for the sake of the compliment. Few men will allow us capacities for their employments."

"It is no compliment to my mind," said Miss Sumelin, and so will ladies think the remainder of this century, let Mrs. Wolstoncraft say what she will.

Bage's sympathy with feminism pervades the action as well as the sentiments of the characters — Miss Fluart's independence and vivacity occupy a prominent place in the novel. It is she who, in replying to Sir John Wing's question as to why the ladies are not seen more in the company at Grondale Hall, makes the witty rejoinder:

Enquire of Lord Grondale, Sir; he does us the honor of protecting us. Our obligations to men are infinite. Under the name of father, or brother, or guardian, or husband, they are always protecting us from liberty.

Bage's criticisms of upper-class selfishness and bourgeois

narrow-mindedness are part of a total outlook which finds its expression in radical political ideas. But in this *Hermsprong* is less rhetorical, more restrained, than the anti-Burkeian parts of *Man as He Is*. Mr. Sumelin's political outlook is certainly unorthodox:

In his youth he had been much abroad, and had looked at men and women of great varieties of colour, modes, and manners. He had even looked at kings and queens, — at lamas, bonzes, and muftis; and having compared and considered what they might, could, or should have done, with what they did, he could not always determine, whether they were delegates from heaven above, or from the earth below; or whether mankind had arrived at its ultimate of perfection and happiness, under any church or any state, or under any alliance between them. That is a heterodoxy most abhorred, I own; and I am sorry it should exist in any of these my people; but truth being a necessary evil in this world sometimes, a poor biographer has not the right to dispense with it, as have the distinguished personages whom I shall always look up to as my divinities here on earth.

But the irony which Glen uses here in describing Mr. Sumelin's eccentricity is discreet in its antimonarchism. However, Hermsprong's political outlook is sufficiently radical for Lord Grondale to hope to be able to prosecute him successfully. The lawyer Corrow explains to his lordship:

He has read the Rights of Man — this I can almost prove; and also that he has lent it to one friend, if not more, which, you know, my Lord, is circulation, though to no great extent. I know also where he said, that the French constitution, though not perfect, had good things in it; and that ours was not so good but it might be mended. Now, you know, my Lord, the bench of Justices will not bear such things now; and if your Lordship will exert your influence, I dare say they will make the country too hot to hold him.

In this way Bage refers to the widespread antiradical activities of the time.

However, at this point in the novel the Cornish miners rise against their masters (who include Grondale). Hermsprong goes among them, but — and evidence of this helps to obtain his acquittal when tried — far from preaching radicalism, exerts all his energies to bring the rising to an end. He speaks to the men sympathetically but firmly:

My friends, we cannot all be rich; there is no possible *equality* of *property* which can last a *day*. If you were capable of desiring it, which I hope you are not, you must wade through such scenes of guilt and horror to obtain it, as you would tremble to speak of. You must finish the horrid conflict by destroying each other.

Events in France since the Revolution, including the Terror, may lie behind these remarks. Hermsprong even goes on to remind the crowd, in terms reminiscent of conservative moralists, of the dangers of wealth:

And why should you desire it? The rich have luxurious tables and disease; if you have poverty, you have health. Add but content, and you have all that is worth having here.

These views had a respectable history among Christian and neo-Stoic moralists insistent upon the demoralizing effects of wealth, but the miners, not surprisingly, are unimpressed. They begin to suspect Hermsprong of being "one of King George's spies, and no better than your master." Hermsprong replies to this charge by knocking down its utterer, to whom he gives half-a-crown and an explanation:

"My good friend," said he, "I am sorry to have hurt you. Anything you had said relative to myself, I should not have so resented; but to revile your *King,* is to weaken the *concord* that ought to exist betwixt him and all his *subjects,* and to overthrow all *civil* order."

These Burkeian sentiments would seem more fitting in the mouth of one of Disraeli's heroes. Here the reader expects irony — perhaps related to the use of italics — but the effect is confused, since the rest of the argument is an appeal to the economic facts:

My friends, perhaps it may be true that your wages are not adequate to the furnishing you with all the superfluities of life which you may desire; but these are unhappy times, and require of you a greater degree of frugality and forbearance.

M. Vitoux has suggested that this passage may reflect Bage's own arguments to his employees in the inflationary period of the French War.[12] It is unsatisfactory because the reader does not know if and where irony is operative in it. It is useful for the plot, in that it makes Hermsprong's acquittal a matter of course, but it is not consistent with, say, Mr. Sumelin's view of monarchy. It may well reflect Bage's uncertainty about the attitude of his publisher and the reading public at the time to tendentious political ideas.[13] Bage is certainly not anarchistic or revolutionary in his sentiments; Hermsprong tries to reestablish order, and gives money to an honest-looking man in the crowd to distribute to the needy:

"There is honesty in your face. I am sure you will dispose of it among those who want, and want the most."
   The man flattered with the distinction, withdrew to a neighbouring ale-house; and bribing a few of the most forward, and giving ale to the others, he prevailed on them to disperse.

So does reality resist the efforts of the idealists; but all is quiet the next day.
   Bage's lack of revolutionary sentiment does not imply the abandonment of his earlier radical views. For his radicalism always had as its basis the preparedness to face facts, the preference for an empirical to a theoretical or conventional approach. The recent events in France must not be ignored, but neither must they be exaggerated. This is Hermsprong's response when Mr. Sumelin raises the topic:

S: "They are going on there in a strange way."
H: "Yes, strange and new. I speak of the causes which animate the French; for as to the means — the destruction of the human species — it has been a favourite mode with power of every denomination, ever since power was."
S: "What are these causes you speak of?"
H: "To make mankind wiser and better."
S: "And do you approve the means?"
H: "What, all? Oh no! It is left to the loyal Englishman, and is, I am told, a new prerogative, — to approve by the lump. All! no, Sir! All the malignant, as well as the better passions, are afloat in France; and malignant actions are the consequence. Many of the acts of the assembly are acts of necessity; and some, no doubt, of folly."

The open mind, as distinct from the capacity "to approve by the lump," is of the essence of Bage's radicalism. Its rarity in contemporary England he deplores, through Glen's comments about a pleasant evening spent with Hermsprong and Woodcock:

So the rest of the evening was spent with chearfulness, the conversation
turning principally on the everlasting subjects, metaphysics and politics;
of the first of which man can *know* nothing, — and of the last, will not. At
least it is so in England, at the moment I am now writing; the order of the
day, as they say in France, being determined ignorance.

"You have, no doubt, Sir, read with attention the author you now so lib-
erally abuse?"

"I, Sir! — I read him! — No, Sir — nor the Mackintoshes, the Flowers,
or the Christies; — I never read a line in any of them — nor ever will."[14]

"It is the way, Sir, to be well informed."

Bage succeeds in retaining his good humor in thus rendering a
perennial antiliberal attitude, to which he was no doubt exposed at
the time. It is because he sees America as a more tolerant country
that Hermsprong prefers it to England. He explains his objection
thus to Miss Fluart:

"It is your politics, Madam; a subject on which the English people delight
to dwell; on which no two people ever thought wholly alike; and on which
you have brought yourselves to so charming a degree of rancour, that you
can bear no deviations from your own opinions. . . . This it is that deforms
your societies; or, to preserve your tempers, and politeness, drives you to
insipidity and cards."

"Are these things better in America?" Miss Fluart asked.

"I think they are. . . . To your polite hatred for opinion, generally they
are strangers. I imagine they owe this to their diversity of religions, which,
accustoming them to see difference of opinion in a matter of the greatest
importance, disposes them to tolerate it on all subjects, and even to believe
it a condition of human nature."

Tolerance takes its place with rationality and benevolence among
the most highly esteemed virtues. It is therefore fitting that conversation on a variety of subjects, which is the practice of toleration
and rationality, should be a notably successful feature of the novel.
In his discussions Bage embodies the radical idea of free thought
and respect for various points of view which are the essence of his
whole outlook.

The idea of progress is one which, both because of Hermsprong's
peculiar background and of its contemporary interest, naturally
comes under discussion (as it had already in *Man as He Is*). Woodcock and Glen argue that Europe is in a state of improvement;
Hermsprong questions this:

"I allow your progressive state," Mr. Hermsprong answered; "and if you will have it, that all is improvement, be it so. You have built cities, no doubt, and filled them full of improvement, if magnificence be improvement; and of poverty also, if poverty be improvement. But our question, my friend, is happiness, comparative happiness; and until you can trace its dependence upon wealth, it will be in vain for you to boast your riches."

To Woodcock's view that Europeans have all the sources of satisfaction open to savages, together with the additional pleasures of art and science, Hermsprong replies that the rich European is often the victim of *taedium vitae* which neither art nor science can cure, and which is unknown to the savage. He agrees that he would not readily dispense with the pleasure of reading, but argues that the Indian may be more healthily employed in sport, and that the variety of a European's reading may often make him confused and superficial. His argument here seems ingenious rather than convincing, and he has modified his position by the time that the topic comes under discussion again. This occurs during dinner at the Sumelins', when the host questions Hermsprong closely:

"Have you in any country seen happiness more diffused than in England?"

"If by happiness you mean money, I think not."

"Money produces the conveniences of life, and its comforts; these produce happiness."

"It produces also the pride, the vanity, the parade of life; and these, if I mistake not, produce in their consequences, a tolerable quantity of anxieties; and anxiety is not happiness."

"To depreciate money is to depreciate commerce, its mother; this the English will not bear."

"I know it well; but I suppose there may be too much even of good things."

"We say, the more commerce, the more prosperity."

"This is changing the idea. Individual happiness was the question; not national prosperity. Your debts and other blessings flowing from the best of all possible governments, impose upon you the necessity of being the first workshop of the world. You labour incessantly for happiness. If you find it, it is well. But savages, like me, have no idea of the happiness of incessant labour."

Here Bage lightly and deftly draws attention to still-unanswered questions about ends and means; about the paradoxical but seemingly inescapable relationship between anxiety and affluence. In this discussion, Hermsprong is more prepared than before to admit the deficiencies of savage life in respect of "intellectual pleasure." There are certain possible improvements for savages as for civilized men:

> "Give them to multiply the objects of their reflection; and to extend the powers of their mind. That, to me, should seem the happiest state of society in which all its members had the power, so to alternate the employments of the mind and body, that the operations of each might be enjoyable. So would the rich man's curse be avoided, that of not knowing what to do with himself; and the poor man's also, that of knowing it but too well."
>
> "And where is this state of society to be found?"
>
> "Alas! nowhere, — not even in America."

There is a clear-sighted awareness of the gap between ideal and reality, but the ideal of rationality and tolerance is nevertheless established convincingly. The lively feminist Miss Fluart and the pragmatic banker Mr. Sumelin have as much right to attention as Hermsprong; no single orthodoxy is imposed.

Conversation is a strong point of the novel even when no serious issue is at stake. Such a minor character as Tom Tunny, the landlord of the Golden Ball, who had "served under Marshal Keith"[15] (as he frequently reminds his customers), is solidly realized through his talk. He has no parallel in the earlier novels, and adds substance to the context in which Hermsprong operates. Hermsprong, in the presence of the curate Woodcock, gently teases Tunny about his military prowess:

> "Englishmen are lions with beer, and heroes with brandy. The field of battle is the bed of honor; and I dare say Mr. Tunny has a thousand times regretted the not lying in it with Marshal Keith."
>
> "Curse me if I have though," says honest Thomas. "No, Sir; I have attacked a battery, and stormed a breach; I have seen death all around and about me; but to tell you a secret, the devil take me, if ever I wished him an inch nearer."
>
> "The sentiment is so natural," said the Curate, "one may rely upon the truth of it, without swearing."
>
> "Why, as to the swearing," returned the landlord, "it's as natural to a soldier as praying to a parson; a soldier has not a bit less religion for it in his heart."

It is Tom Tunny also who makes the appropriate criticism of Dr.

Blick, when he breaks the rules of conversation by embarking on a harangue against "the abominable doctrines of the French philosophers." Tunny first falls asleep and, when awakened, defends himself:

"Doctor," says the landlord, "I always thought a pulpit a fitter place to preach in than an alehouse; and that a man must fall asleep when he cannot keep himself awake. It is not orthodox here to preach over our liquor."

The comedy again serves Bage's overall purpose.

Bage was well aware that the attitude of tolerant common sense which he was trying to convey was very unlike that which pervaded the most popular novels of the day, in which sensationalism and sensibility were the chief sources of interest. He refers satirically to both fashions. When Miss Fluart and Miss Campinet are leaving Grondale for Falmouth, Bage comments on the dangers of the journey:

All ladies know, — for all ladies read novels — how extremely dangerous the roads of England are for female travellers, who happen to be young and handsome. The banditti who infest these roads, are of the higher order of mortal men, such as seldom arrive at the gallows, whatsoever may be the pains they take to do it; lords, knights and gentle squires.

The ladies, however, escape the attentions of these romantic novelists' *banditti*[16] and reach Falmouth without adventure. Bage's reference to the cult of sensibility is more direct and dismissive. It occurs when he is discussing the effect of the revelation about Hermsprong's birth upon Lord Grondale:

It may indeed be possible, that we may be good stoics still, when the misfortunes of our friends call upon us for firmness in adversity; but in our own, our sensibility is quite as keen as any reasonable person ought to desire. I meddle not with that other sort of sensibility, so fashionable, and so pretty to talk about, because I begin to be of opinion, it was made only to be talked about; having watched it ever since it was born, and never having yet seen it rob a man of his appetite, or steal a rose from the fair cheek of beauty.

This amused awareness of the excesses of contemporary literary attitudes confirms the sense that the novel gives throughout of being the expression of a sane and balanced outlook, which makes use of its improbable hero for well-considered ends.

IV   *Success*

Hermsprong was deservedly the most successful of Bage's six novels. Despite its unorthodox sentiments, seven editions were published between 1796 and 1828.[17] It has also appeared in two twentieth-century editions from the Turnstile Press in 1951 with a thoughtful and enthusiastic introduction by Mr. Vaughan Wilkins, and from the Folio Society in 1960 in a handsome illustrated edition. Professor Stuart Tave is now editing it for the Oxford English Novels series.

The early reviews revealed differences of political outlook between the reviewers, as considered in Chapter 1. Twentieth-century commentators have been equally varied in their responses. Walter Allen has called Bage "a doctrinaire novelist proper" on the strength of this novel, because of its "completely intransigent attack on feudalism and the notion of aristocracy,"[18] and J. M. S. Tompkins regards *Hermsprong* as differing from Bage's earlier novels in being less eclectic and speculative and more "tendentious" and diagrammatic.[19] Similarly, J. H. Sutherland distinguishes between Bage's earlier "novels of ideas," where a number of points of view were shown sympathetically, as in Peacock, and his later "liberal didactic novels," more akin to those of Holcroft and Godwin.[20] Nevertheless Sutherland insists that Bage still retains a certain detachment and breadth of sympathy, a "civilized tolerance and understanding of the relativity of ideas."[21] Vaughan Wilkins puts this point of view more firmly, claiming that Bage is not a propagandist but, like Peacock, "a detached and cultivated observer."[22]

Divergent views are possible because *Hermsprong* combines the ironical tone of detachment with a plot based on strong moral contrasts. Gregory Glen's sympathies are shared by the reader. Tolerance is highly valued, but it is not extended to those who are themselves intolerant. The reader is aware of the arrogance and conceit of Lord Grondale and Sir Philip Chestrum, and the sycophancy of Dr. Blick, but the interest of the novel is not exhausted by the contrast between them and the more sympathetic characters. What matters more — and gives the fullest expression to Bage's radicalism — is our sense of the vitality and humanity of the values repre-

sented by Hermsprong, Glen, Woodcock, Mr. Sumelin, and Miss
Fluart. The didactic moralist may all too easily reduce his world to
a lucidly lifeless contrast between the rejected and the applauded.
The variety among Bage's good characters here, Mr. Sumelin con-
ducting his witty and unsuccessful campaign against his wife's
adamantine worldliness, Miss Fluart encouraging Lord Grondale's
affections and maneuvering to keep them within the bounds of
decorum. Hermsprong gaining Miss Sumelin's undying hatred by
the purity of his behavior toward her; the rendering in conversations of a lively flow of ideas on many topics of current, and sometimes continuing, concern; the sympathy for American institutions,
for feminism, for an undogmatic religious view; these features, uni-
fied by the light and flexible tone, create a successful novel of radical ideas: idealistic, sensible, and entertaining.

CHAPTER 8

Reputation and Achievement

I Early Reputation

I T has been seen that Bage was received with modest praise by most of his reviewers, and the fact that three of his novels were pirated in Dublin, and three achieved second editions, supports the idea of some success. *Man as He Is* was issued by the Minerva Press in 1792, 1796, and 1819, while *Hermsprong* appeared from the Minerva Press in 1796 and 1799, was pirated in Dublin in 1796, and was issued by Mrs. Barbauld in her collection *The British Novelists* in 1810 and 1820 and by the Chiswick Press, in a very elegant edition, in 1828.[1]

This is the more impressive in that the liberal and radical ideas which Bage expressed became increasingly unfashionable in the early nineteenth century:

"Jacobinism is killed and gone," declared Sheridan, who had himself joined Addington's Ministry, in December 1802: "And by whom? By him who can no longer be called the child and champion of Jacobinism; by Buonaparté."[2]

The Terror in Paris turned many Englishmen against the French Revolution and seemed to confirm Burke's eloquent warnings. And especially after Napoleon became Emperor of the French in 1804, the war with France could be seen as a defense of freedom against oppression, and liberal notions condemned as symptoms of unpatriotic Jacobinism.

Thus it is not surprising that Mrs. Barbauld should have been cautious in her support of Bage in her "Preface, biographical and critical" to her 1810 edition of *Hermsprong*. She refers to Bage as "the author of several novels which have met with a favourable reception from the public,'' discusses his remoteness from ''fashionable or literary circles,'' and places the novel in its period:

Hermsprong is democratical in its tendency. It was published at a time when sentiments of that nature were prevalent with a large class of people, and was much read. It has some strength of thought; but it is far from being a regular work, or exhibiting a consistent character. *Man as He Is* has more of a story, and more variety of character.[3]

Reasons are then given for considering the earlier novel the better, mostly concerning the characterization of Lady Paradyne — ''drawn with some humour,'' and Miss Carlill — ''the author has exceedingly well hit off the acuteness and presence of mind, and coolness in argument, by which the society she is supposed to belong to are so much distinguished.''[4] The conclusion is balanced but approving:

The whole is the work of a man who knows the world; and has reflected upon what he has seen; of a man whose mind has more strength than elegance; and whose opinions, often just, sometimes striking, are marked with traits of singularity, and not infrequently run counter to received notions and established usages.[5]

Mrs. Barbauld's is a judiciously sympathetic account. No explanation is given of her choosing to republish a novel of Bage's which she did not consider his best; she wished either to speak up in this indirect way for ''democratical'' principles, or to represent Bage by his best-known book.

The early nineteenth century witnessed a considerable change of attitude in English society, with a growing emphasis on respectability and delicacy, despite the careers of Byron and the Prince Regent. The influence of the Evangelical movement as embodied in public figures like William Wilberforce (who had been one of the sponsors of the Royal Proclamation against Vice and Immorality in 1787), gradually affected English manners and attitudes. This process has been amusingly described by Muriel Jaeger in *Before Victoria,* which shows how thoroughly, by 1837, ''Victorianism had already prepared the way for Victoria.''[6]

The growing ''delicacy'' of the period is discussed by the Victorian historian Lord Mahon in his *History of England 1713–83,* especially in the chapter on ''Life and Manners'' in the seventh volume. Mahon records an anecdote about Scott's grand-aunt who found herself shocked when trying to reread Aphra Behn:

"Take back your bonny Mrs. Behn," said Mrs. Keith, "and if you would follow my advice, put her in the fire. But is it not a strange thing," she added, "that I, a woman of eighty, sitting alone, feel myself ashamed to look through a book which, sixty years ago, I have heard read aloud for the amusement of large circles of the best company in London?"[7]

Mahon notes how the "wavering taste of the public in the matters of such liberties as Fielding's" was finally turned against him by the advent of Miss Burney, "because the subjects on which she dwelt were more nearly the same as Fielding's ... without even a single line unfit to meet a young lady's eye, or unworthy to proceed from a young lady's hand."[8] The autobiography of Mrs. Schimmelpenninck, the daughter of Samuel Galton of the Lunar Society, furnishes confirmation of the extent of the change. The elderly Mrs. Schimmelpenninck, who was born in 1778, looked back from Victorian England in 1858 on the lamentable period when the novels of Fielding and Smollett had "desecrated the library shelves."[9] She went on:

How great an obligation do we owe to Sir Walter Scott for raising the tone of light literature, and infusing into it, not only much instruction and information, but noble and elevated sentiments, and a tone of feeling honourable, manly, highly moral, and to a certain degree Christian! None but those aged as I myself, and who recollect the past condition of things, can appreciate the full debt we owe him.[10]

It is against this background that Scott's account of Bage in his "Biographical Memoir" in 1824, the only substantial early critical essay, must be set.

II   Scott's View

Scott gives an accurate account of the kind of novels that Bage wrote:

The general effect of Bage's compositions, is rather to exhibit character, than to compose a narrative; rather to extend and infuse his own political and philosophical opinions, in which a man of his character was no doubt sincere, than merely to amuse the reader with the wonders, or melt him with the sorrows, of a fictitious tale.[11]

In this, and in his "quaint, facetious, ironical style," Bage is held to be close to such French didactic novelists as Diderot and Voltaire.[12] Scott then goes on to make clear his disagreement with "the tendency and motive of those works.[13] Bage was probably brought up as a Quaker, but "he appears to have wandered ... into the wastes of scepticism,"[14] while his political outlook may have been "biassed by the frequent visits of the excisemen, who levied taxes on his commodities, for the purpose of maintaining a war which he disapproved of."[15] He may also have shared the French view that "persons of literary attainments" should contribute to the forming of systems of government[16] — a view not reasonably taken in a country with a free press, used to hearing both sides of an argument.

Scott comments acutely on the limitations of the didactic novel:

It is a kind of composition more adapted to confirm those who hold similar opinions with the author, by affording them a triumph at the expense of their opponents, than to convince those who may be disposed calmly to investigate the subject.[17]

He also criticizes Bage's treatment of both the upper and lower social classes. His rich men are generally ogres, whereas (in Scott's view) the prevailing vice of the rich is their "apathy"; and his poor men exhibit habits of "virtue and generosity," whereas in fact "the hardness of their situation often leads them to recklessness" and "to extend the circle of their pleasures, at the expense of their morals."[18] Thus, for Scott, the happiest social state is the intermediate one. In fact, this is the view which Bage, too, takes care to impart through all his novels.

It is, however, in the treatment of sexual morality that Scott finds Bage to be most seriously at fault, exhibiting "a dangerous tendency to slacken the rein of discipline upon a point where, perhaps, of all others, society must be benefitted by their curbing restraint."[19] On this theme Scott becomes increasingly eloquent. Where Fielding and Smollett had allowed their heroes to be "rakes and debauchees," Bage "extended that licence to females" and "seems at times even to sport with ties of marriage."[20] Scott agrees that it is possible to imagine someone like Kitty Ross in *Barham*

Downs being seduced "under circumstances so peculiar as to excite great compassion," and therefore being eventually admissible again into society as "a humble penitent."[21] But even so, she would have to be constantly reminded of her fall:

Her disgrace must not be considered as a trivial stain, which may be communicated by a husband as an exceeding good jest to his friend and correspondent; there must be, not penitence and reformation alone, but humiliation and abasement, in the recollection of her errors. This the laws of society demand even from the unfortunate; and to compromise further, would open a door to the most unbounded licentiousness.[22]

Scott is here magisterially expressing that view of the purity of women as the basis of social stability which was to become characteristic of the Victorian middle class, and which underlies the treatment of the heroines in Scott's own novels and those of Dickens and Thackeray.

Scott is less concerned about Bage's "indelicacy of expression," which he attributes to "the faulty example of earlier novelists," and has "to some degree chastened in the present edition."[23] More important, and dangerous, in Scott's view, are Bage's beliefs about human behavior and the foundation of moral conduct, as most clearly seen in *Hermsprong*. Scott quotes Wordsworth's "A reasoning, self-sufficient thing, an intellectual all-in-all" as hitting off the type, and doubts both whether such a man could exist and whether such "practical philosophy" could lead to the good life:

Let each reader ask his own bosom, whether it were possible for him to hold an unaltered tenor of moral and virtuous conduct, did he suppose that to himself alone he was responsible, and that his own reason, a judge so peculiarly subject to be bribed, blinded and imposed upon by the sophistry with which the human mind can gloss over those actions to which human passions so strongly impel us, was the ultimate judge of his actions?[24]

If the reader says yes, he is either "a faultless monster" or a self-deceiver. Scott argues that unaided reason failed to provide the ancients with a satisfactory basis for their ethics, instancing the grossness and license satirized by Juvenal, Petronius, and Lucian. If similar licentiousness has not followed the repudiation of religion in modern times, this is due to the surviving legacy of Christian morality. Scott ends by suggesting that "the philosophic Square" in *Tom Jones* is a truer representation of a follower of Reason than is Hermsprong.[25]

Scott's indignation has now passed its meridian. He does not believe that Bage behaved immorally, despite the "speculative errors" which may have resulted from his attachment to Quaker beliefs. No doubt Bage acted with the uprightness of Arnold and Miss Carlill, who represent the best aspects of "these interesting and primitive persons."[26] Scott can now turn to the "high and decided merit" of the novels, which he discerns in the characterization and dialogue, and insight into "the internal working of a powerful understanding, like Paracelsus Holman," and the "light, gay, pleasing air," the "ease and good humour of the style."[27] For these reasons, Scott has included Bage in his series:

> We did not think it proper to reject the work of so eminent an author from the collection, merely on account of speculative errors.[28]

The reader is left to be amused by the novels, safely, because Scott does not believe that "the youngest and most thoughtless derive their serious opinions from works of this nature."[29] Nevertheless, somewhat uneasily, perhaps, Scott concludes with the reminder that "a good jest is no argument."[30]

Scott's estimate of Bage, as one of the editors of the *Lives of the Novelists* has noted, is the most unorthodox view expressed therein. Croker, and Scott's other friends of the *Quarterly Review* and the *Edinburgh Review,* as G. S. suggests, must have been surprised at his choice of "the eccentric and unpopular Bage"[31] — although the unpopularity must not be exaggerated. It may have been a concession on Scott's part to the likely views of his literary associates that he chose to republish three of the earlier and less Jacobin novels rather than *Hermsprong,* which he asserted to be the best — in this way curiously reversing the behavior of Mrs. Barbauld. Thus, although Scott's attitude to Bage's sexual morality and politics is, to the modern reader, strikingly conventional and conservative, his discussion of Bage as a whole reveals Scott's fundamental fair-mindedness — the quality which enabled him to create the balance of sympathies in, for example, *Waverley.* Scott's moderation becomes even clearer when it is contrasted with the response it elicited from the *Quarterly Review.*

III   *Other Criticism*

In 1825 Galignani in Paris detached the introductory essays from the unsuccessful *Novelist's Library* and published them as *The Lives of the Novelists*. The review of this in the *Quarterly Review* the following year begins with a survey of the rise of the novel, associating it with literacy, and takes issue with Scott over his minimizing the moral influence of literature and being overindulgent to *Tom Jones*. But Scott is praised, not altogether accurately, for his severe treatment of "a very inferior novelist," Robert Bage:

> The writer whose works have thus been recalled from an oblivion which we cannot help thinking they merited, wrote at the period of the French Revolution; and though he had been born and bred among the primitive and virtuous set of our quakers, he systematically made his novels the vehicle of all the anti-social, anti-moral and anti-religious theories that were then but too much in vogue among the half-educated classes in this country. Sir Walter, after exposing with just ridicule the style of gross and senseless caricature in which Mr. Bage, the son of a miller, and himself a paper-maker in a little country town, has thought fit to paint the manners of English gentlemen and ladies, proceeds ... to notice the far graver offences of which his pen had been guilty.[32]

The *Quarterly* concludes sadly:

> It is, in truth, a melancholy reflection how largely the works, not of Bage merely, but of the true classics of the English Novel, stand in need of being introduced with preliminary caution such as we have now been quoting.[33]

The reviewer's indignation throws into relief Scott's wider sympathies.

The moralizing mood was not, indeed, universal. For in striking and welcome contrast to the acerbity of the *Quarterly* is the view of *Hermsprong* taken by Henry Crabb Robinson, also in 1825. Crabb Robinson, who knew so many people and read so many books, had been acquainted with Godwin, Holcroft, and William Taylor in the 1790s, but evidently did not know of Bage at that time. For May 18 he noted:

> I read on this walk an excellent novel, *Hermsprong, or Man as He is Not* — the hero an American, a democratic philosopher — a polemical tale in

which Dr. Blick, a parson, and (Lord Grondale), a persecuting, insolent and unjust peer, are exposed. The dialogue rather coarse. Miss Fluart, the pert companion of the heroine, Lord Grondale's daughter, an amusing character. Though I am tired of the doctrines of the book, they are true, and, having read little in that way lately, the book amused me. It is a work of talent by a Mr. Bage.[34]

This comment, especially its reference to the truth of Bage's "doctrine," needs to be put beside the conservative view if we are not to oversimplify the prevailing attitudes of the 1820s, which were clearly diverse.

The Chiswick Press *Hermsprong* in 1828 was the last edition of any of Bage's novels until 1951. It is not surprising that the Victorians should have forgotten or neglected him, since their moral view was similar to Scott's, and they had an increasing number of good novels to read. But there was at least one Victorian reader who thought highly of Bage. In a letter of 1854 Miss Mitford pronounced *Tom Jones* overrated, and in fact inferior to *Humphry Clinker*. She went on:

This is going the rounds of the famous comic romances; but some, not so famous, are much better. I assure you there is no comparison between *Tom Jones* and *Hermsprong,* whether for cleverness or as a matter of mere amusement, allowing always for what 60 years ago was called the mad philosophy. Scott thought of it pretty much as I do.[35]

Miss Mitford's reminiscence of Scott's view is hardly accurate, but her un-Victorian enthusiasm for the novel is remarkable. In her, Muriel Jaeger has argued, may be seen a conflict between the liberal views of the period of her childhood and the narrowness of the new era — "an incessant mental seesaw between the wide and the narrow outlook."[36]

The only major Victorian discussion of Bage was published in *The Reliquary: Quarterly Archaeological Journal and Review*. In July 1869 Henry Kirke, a regular contributor to the magazine, gave an account entitled "Robert Bage — a Derbyshire Worthy." It outlines Bage's life and seems to be based upon Scott's "Prefatory Memoir" — indeed, it follows Scott closely in both order and argument. For instance, Kirke is eloquently indignant about Bage's sexual morality and he criticizes the lack of respect for "religious or political restraint" in *Hermsprong*. Nevertheless, he asserts that "Bage's novels deserve our highest praise," and Bage is finally raised to a provincial pedestal: "He certainly deserves to be placed in the highest rank of Derbyshire Worthies."[37] In general it is evident that the Victorian age, rich in fiction of its own, paid no attention to this unorthodox minor novelist.

The development of modern literary scholarship has redirected attention to Bage, together with many other minor writers, not all worth attention. Walter Raleigh provided the first historical treatment in *The English Novel* in 1894, followed by other historians of the novel like W. L. Cross, George Saintsbury, E. A. Baker, J. M. S. Tompkins, J. R. Foster, Richard Church, Walter Allen, and Lionel Stevenson. Bage also appears in discussions of social and political ideas in the later eighteenth century, particularly in relation to the French Revolution, and in two enthusiastic articles, "A Forgotten Novelist" by Hermione Ramsden in *The Yellow Book* in 1897, and "Robert Bage: A Forgotten Novelist" by Carl H. Grabo in the *Mid-West Quarterly* in 1918. G. Barnett Smith's account of Bage in the *Dictionary of Natural Biography* in 1908, though necessarily largely based on Scott, gave a sympathetic personal view of the novels:

In reality, it was the keenness of his satire that was distasteful to the orthodox, and caused them to brand as dangerous works whose sparkling humour, genuine ability, and in the main generous and elevating sentiments, were not sufficiently recognised.[38]

Barnett Smith thoroughly approved of Scott's having reissued three of the novels, and regretted the absence of a collected edition. So far, only *Hermsprong* has appeared in the twentieth century. The 1951 edition by the Turnstile Press has a lively introduction by Vaughan Wilkins, and produced a sympathetic review from V. S. Pritchett in the *New Statesman;* the Folio Society edition of 1960 has pleasant illustrations by Cecil Keeling. The same novel is forthcoming in the Oxford English Novels series.

So far the most thorough critical accounts of Bage (apart from unpublished theses) are by Harrison R. Steeves in his survey of the eighteenth-century novel, *Before Jane Austen* (1966) and by Gary Kelly in *The English Jacobin Novel* (1976). Professor Steeves' chapter on Bage is entitled "An Eighteenth-Century Shaw," but no attempt is made to press the parallel beyond the fact that both wrote wittily and critically about society. For Professor Steeves Bage promises more than he achieves, and so remains "a fond disappointment," but nevertheless the minor novelist of his time most likely to "provide a tolerant reader with a new and rewarding experience."[39] Gary Kelly considers him worthy to be considered with Godwin, Holcroft, and Mrs. Inchbald as the significant radical novelists of the era.

IV   *The Novel of Ideas: Didactic and Comic Modes*

Bage is an interesting practitioner of the mode usually termed the novel of ideas (in Northrop Frye's terminology, the anatomy), which is sometimes undervalued because it is felt to be outside the central tradition of the novel. Through Philip Quarles in *Point Counter Point,* Aldous Huxley expresses his sense of the limitations of the form:

Novel of ideas. The character of each personage must be implied, as far as possible, in the ideas of which he is the mouthpiece. In so far as theories are rationalisations of sentiments, instincts, dispositions of soul, this is possible.... The great defect of the novel of ideas is that it's a made-up affair. Necessarily; for people who can reel off neatly formulated notions aren't quite real; they're slightly monstrous.[40]

Nevertheless, it was the form that Huxley himself practiced successfully in *Brave New World* and *Island,* and it has never lacked practitioners or readers.

The novelist of ideas may make use of the ideas in different ways, either by recommending one series (the didactic mode), or by balancing and playing off one idea against another (the comic mode). In the eighteenth century Johnson's *Rasselas* and Voltaire's *L'Ingénu* exemplify the didactic mode, though both have elements of comedy. The polarizing of political attitudes over the French Revolution encouraged a similar emphasis. The clearest examples of the didactic novel of ideas at this time would be Godwin's *Caleb Williams* and Holcroft's *Anna St. Ives.* The latter in particular is based on a simple tug-of-war, with the heroine, Anna, sought by both the rakish aristocrat Coke Clifton and the rational moralist Frank Henley. Virtue triumphs in the end; Anna marries Frank, while Clifton is won over by their magnanimity to virtue and good sense; Frank leaves the final scene with a "glowing and hoping heart."

The interest of Bage is that while he undoubtedly held and

expressed radical social views, there is also a strong element of the comic mode in the novels — pleasure taken in exposing the over-simplifications of the intellect through a kind of caricature, the mode practiced most successfully in English by Thomas Love Peacock in the early nineteenth century. Several critics have in fact felt an affinity between Bage and Peacock. Vaughan Wilkins, for example, in his 1951 introduction to *Hermsprong,* called him "a detached and cultivated observer," who must have influenced both Peacock and Jane Austen.[41] J. H. Sutherland in the *Philosophical Quarterly* in 1957 argued on the same lines, stressing their "civilised tolerance and understanding of the relativity of ideas."[42] On the other hand Walter Allen asserted in *The English Novel* in 1954 that Bage is "a doctrinaire novelist proper": "In a sense, with Bage the class-war enters fiction, for *Hermsprong* is a completely intransigent attack on feudalism and the notion of aristocracy."[43] Allen does not refer to Bage's earlier novels, in which the didactic element is less prominent, though by no means unimportant. But even in *Hermsprong* the tone has a lightness and vivacity that contrasts oddly with Allen's suggestion of intransigence. The element of kinship with Peacock is delightfully present; it lies in the amusement which both Bage and Peacock derive from contemplating the ridiculous ideas of some of their contemporaries, and from their common use of discussion as a major constituent of their novels. Both found unpractical theorists absurd, whether they are old Holman and Miss Caradoc in Bage or Lord Curryfin in Peacock; there is a considerable resemblance between such languid aristocrats as Sir Antony Havelly and Lord Bardoe on the one hand and the Hon. Mr. Listless on the other. It is at what he claims to be a Roman camp that the Reverend Dr. Blick first comes across Hermsprong, and it is at a Roman camp that the Reverend Dr. Folliott (a much more likable cleric) discovers Captain Fitzchrome.[44] Yet there is no documentary evidence that Peacock read Bage's novels, however likely it seems that he may have done so. As Howard Mills remarks:

> It is possible to find interesting *parallels* with Lucian, Marmontel, Robert Bage or Isaac D'Israeli, but difficult to find tangible evidence of direct influence, or even of Peacock reading them or owning copies.[45]

Yet the possibility of influence remains. When Mary Shelley was keeping a journal in 1815, she recorded reading two of Bage's novels, first *Hermsprong,* then *Man as He Is.* On 6 April she noted: "Read *Man as He Is.* Hogg comes and reads [Scott's] *Rokeby.* Peacock dines with us. In the evening walk and talk."[46] Did Bage's novels form part of the material for that conversation? The evidence remains inconclusive.

But at all events it is not on his historical influence, which was certainly very small, that any claims for Bage must be based. These must be based on the considerable merits of the novels themselves, especially the last two, which achieve a mature balance between the comic and the didactic modes characteristic of the two potentialities of the novel of ideas. In doing so they throw up for consideration a large number of important questions about social and political issues, in a spirit which is constructive, well balanced, and good-humored. To have maintained that spirit in the 1780s and 1790s was a considerable achievement; nor is it without relevance to our own somber day.

Notes and References

Chapter One

1. The parish register of St. Alkmund's, Derby, records the baptism of Robert, son of George and Mary Bage, on February 26, 1728. Later accounts, however, give the date of birth as February 29. See W. Hutton, "Memoir" in *Monthly Magazine* XIII (1802), 478 (where Hutton remarks that "though he lived to the age of 73, he could not celebrate more than 18 birthdays") and obituary in *Gentleman's Magazine* LXXI (London, 1801), 1206.

2. Hutton, "Memoir," *Monthly Magazine*, XIII, 248.

3. *Ballantyne's Novelist's Library, IX, The Novels of Swift, Bage and Cumberland,* ed. Walter Scott (London, 1824), p. xxvi. See the obituary of Catherine Hutton in the *Birmingham Journal,* March 21, 1846:

She supplied Sir Walter Scott, at his request, with the material for the life of Mr. Bage, of Elford, who, in his day, was an eminent writer of fiction. This contribution appears in the Edinburgh Edition of English Novels, edited by "the Ariosto of the North."

Quoted by Mrs. C. H. Beale, *Reminiscences of a Gentlewoman of the Last Century* (Birmingham, 1891), p. 233.

4. See A. Gregory, *The French Revolution and the English Novel* (London, 1915), p. 173, and especially J. H. Sutherland, "Bage's supposed Quaker Upbringing," in *Notes and Queries* CXCVIII (1953), 32–33.

5. Parish register of St. Alkmund's, Derby, August 3, 1751.

6. In a memorandum in the William Salt Library at Stafford, M. 761/20, dated September 15, 1753, Bage is recorded as having paid to the owners £269 out of £719 due for principal and interest. An agreement had been reached over the outstanding £450 of the principal.

7. Staffordshire County Record Office, "Sale by auction of Fisherwick Park, 15 November, 1804." D. 661/19/10/18.

8. C. Kegan Paul, *William Godwin: His Friends and Contemporaries* (London, 1876), I, 262–63.

9. Hutton, *The Life of William Hutton* (London, 1816), p. 77.

10. *Ibid.,* p. 97.

11. Kegan Paul, *Godwin,* I, 263.

12. For a scholarly account of Darwin, see D. King-Hele, *Erasmus Darwin, 1731–1802* (London, 1963).

13. The eldest, Charles, was baptized at St. Alkmund's, Derby, February 8, 1752. The two younger sons were baptized at St. Peter's, Elford, Edward on January 1, 1755, and John on October 28, 1758.

14. Hutton, "Memoir," *Monthly Magazine,* XIII, 278.

15. Kegan Paul, *Godwin,* I, 263.

16. Hutton, "Memorandums from memory," Mss. in Birmingham Public Library, March 28, 1761, p. 18.

17. Hutton, "Memoir," *Monthly Magazine,* XIII, 479.

18. The deed of sale, dated July 21, 1766, is preserved in the William Salt Library at Stafford:

Robert Bage consents to sell to the Right Honourable the Earl of Donegal All his Estate at Elford consisting of one Corn Mill, one Paper Mill, with their fixed appurtenances, Two Houses, One Drying Room, three Warehouses, Stables, etc. for £2,000. . . .
The Earl of Donegal lets for the term of 61 years to Robert Bage the Mill etc. for £46 p.a.

Mss. M 761/20.

19. Dorothy Stroud, *Capability Brown* (London, 1950), p. 92.

20. Haliday to Lord Marchmont, June 21, 1788; quoted in G. E. C., *The Complete Peerage,* IV (London, 1916), 392.

21. *Ibid.,* p. 392.

22. William Pitt, *A General View of the Agriculture of the County of Stafford,* Second edition (London, 1813), p. 257.

23. Hutton, *History of Derby* (1791). Second edition (Birmingham, 1817), p. 249.

24. Scott, "Prefatory Memoir," p. xxv.

25. *Ibid.,* p. xxiv.

26. *Ibid.,* p. xxiv.

27. William Pitt, *A Topographical History of Staffordshire* (Newcastle under Lyme, 1817), pp. 132–33.

28. *Ibid.,* p. 133.

29. Hutton, *History of Birmingham* (1782). Sixth edition (Birmingham, 1835), p. 67.

30. Conrad Gill, *History of Birmingham* (Oxford, 1952), I, 120.

31. See W. K. V. Gale, *Boulton, Watt and the Soho Undertakings* (Birmingham, 1952) *passim.*

32. Hutton, *Birmingham,* p. 398.

33. F.A. Wendeborn, *A View of England Towards the Close of the Eighteenth Century* (London, 1791), I, 229. The Preface explains that it was originally published in German and translated by the author to avoid being pirated.

34. Asa Briggs, *The Age of Improvement* (London, 1959), p. 45.

35. See R. E. Schofield, *The Lunar Society of Birmingham* (Oxford, 1963), esp. Parts II and III.

36. *Ibid.,* p. 440.

37. Leonard Horner, *Memoirs and Correspondence,* II, 2; quoted by Samuel Smiles, *Lives of Boulton and Watt* (London, 1865), Ch. XVIII.

38. J. Priestley, *Memoirs of Dr. Joseph Priestley* (London, 1806), I, 97.

39. Smiles, *Boulton and Watt,* p. 413.

40. Bage, *Man as He Is* (London, 1792), II, 216.

41. Miss Beale, *Reminiscences of a Gentlewoman,* p. 71.

42. Priestley, *Memoirs,* I, 98.

43. Gill, *Birmingham,* I, 142–43.

44. *A Catalogue of the Books Belonging to the Birmingham Library* (Birmingham, 1795). Pages unnumbered. Holcroft was an active radical writer and friend of Godwin. J. H. Bernardin de St. Pierre was the best-known disciple of Rousseau, and his *Chaumière indienne* appeared in 1791. It was translated in the same year by R. A. Kendall. In the catalogue for 1798, there appear also Day's *Sandford and Merton* and some of the *contes* of Voltaire, in translation in the *Novelists' Magazine,* including "Zadig" in Vol. II and "The Sincere Huron" in Vol. XXI.

45. Hutton, *Birmingham,* p. 160.

46. William Salt Library, Stafford, Mss. M. 761 / 20.

47. Kegan Paul, *Godwin,* I, 263 (there is no Darwin record which corroborates this).

48. Hutton, "Memoir," *Monthly Magazine,* XIII, 479.

49. Kegan Paul, *Godwin,* I, 263.

50. S. MacCoby, *The English Radical Tradition 1763–1914* (London, 1952), p. 1.

51. E. P. Thompson, *The Making of the English Working Class* (1963; Harmondsworth, 1968), p. 26.

52. Edmund Burke, *Reflections on the Revolution in France* (1790), ed. W. B. Todd (New York, 1965), p. 105.

53. William Godwin, *Enquiry Concerning Political Justice* (1793), ed. F. E. L. Priestley (Toronto, 1946), I, 181.

54. A. O. Aldridge, *Man of Reason* (London, 1959), p. 8.

55. Mary Wollstonecraft, *A Vindication of the Rights of Woman* (1792), ed. Miriam Kramnick (Harmondsworth, 1975), p. 92.

56. F. Copleston, *A History of Philosophy,* VI (London, 1960), 419.

57. See A. Lincoln, *Some Political and Social Ideas of English Dissent 1763–1800* (Cambridge, 1938), Chs. IV and V.

58. Quoted in MacCoby, *The English Radical Tradition,* p. 54, from Price's "Discourse on the Love of Our Country" (1789).

59. Early essays by Paine in the *Pennsylvania Magazine* (1775) are "Duelling" and "Reflections on Titles"; see *The Complete Writings of Thomas Paine* ed. Philip S. Foner (New York, 1945), [II] 28–32 , 33–34. Paine also condemned titles in *The Rights of Man* (1791); Foner, *Paine* [I],

286–87. Godwin has chapters of Book V of his *Enquiry* entitled "Moral Effects of Aristocracy," "Of Titles," and "Of the Aristocratical Character."

60. G. Kelly, *The English Jacobin Novel 1780–1805,* (Oxford, 1976), p. 8.

61. *The Anti-Jacobin Review and Magazine,* V, (Feb. 1800), p. 152.

62. Kegan Paul, *Godwin,* I, 263.

63. Ibid., I, 263, and Hutton, "Memoir," *Monthly Magazine,* XIII, 479.

64. See H. R. Steeves, "The Date of Bage's *Mount Henneth,"* *Notes and Queries* N.S. XII, 1 (Jan. 1965), 27.

65. *Monthly Review,* LXVI (Feb. 1782), 130.

66. *The Autobiography of Leigh Hunt* (1850), ed. J. Morpurgo (London, 1949), p. 47.

67. J. M. S. Tompkins, *The Popular Novel in England 1770–1800* (London, 1932), p. 1.

68. E. A. Osborne, "A Preliminary Survey for a Bibliography of the Novels of Robert Bage," in *Book Handbook,* ed. R. Horrox (Bracknell, Berks, 1951), p. 31.

69. *Monthly Review* LXXVII (April 1787), 325-26.

70. *Monthly Review* LXXX (June 1789), 502.

71. *Critical Review* LXVII (Jan. 1789), 76.

72. *European Magazine* XIV (Dec. 1788), 416.

73. Charles Lamb, "The Sanity of True Genius," in *Last Essays of Elia,* Enfield Edition, IV (London, 1875), 27. Quoted by Dorothy Blakey, *The Minerva Press 1790–1820* (London, 1939), p. 62. This is a thorough account of the Press, with much useful information on William Lane.

74. Lane supported the Ministry at the 1788 election, and by 1791 he was a Lieutenant Colonel in the Honourable Artillery Company's White Regiment. He became the first Captain of the West London Regiment of the militia in 1794. In the same year he announced that the Press would "never convey to the happy subjects of this kingdom false founded doctrines or opinions, but, attached to the prosperity of the country, it [would] be a bastion for its support." See Blakey, *Minerva Press,* pp. 19ff. One wonders whether Lane actually read Bage's novels before publishing them.

75. Hutton, "Memoir," *Monthly Magazine* XIII, 479.

76. Birmingham Public Library, Local Studies Library, MSS 486802. Aug. 1, 1787; the letter is quoted by Scott in his "prefatory Memoir," p. xix. But the text printed by Scott of this and other letters had evidently been tidied up by Catherine Hutton to accord with the stricter habits of the new century.

77. Birmingham MSS. 23 Feb. 1789; Scott, "Prefatory Memoir," p. xx.

78. Now in the Derby Public Library.

79. See Eric Robinson 'The Derby Philosophical Society,' in A. E. Musson and Eric Robinson, *Science and Technology in the Industrial Revolution* (Manchester, 1969), 190–99.

80. Hutton, *History of Derby,* (1791), "Eminent Men." Second edition (London), 1817, pp. 247–49.

81. Schofield, *Lunar Society,* p. 358.

82. Gill, *Birmingham,* I, 146.

83. Hutton, *Life* (1816), p. 194. The section is entitled "A Narrative of the Riots in Birmingham, July 14, 1791. Particularly as they affected the Author."

84. *Ibid.,* 195.

85. Birmingham Mss. 25 July 1791.

86. *Ibid.,* 11 Aug. 1791.

87. *Ibid.,* 14 April 1792. Bage evidently appeared as a witness for Hutton in court; see letters in Hutton-Beale Collection 29A-B in Birmingham Public Library.

88. Matthew Boulton to Charles Dumergue, 18 Aug. 1791. Quoted by Schofield, *Lunar Society,* p. 362.

89. Birmingham Mss. Undated.

90. *The Correspondence of William Cowper,* ed. T. Wright (London, 1904), IV, 387–88. March 1793.

91. *Ibid.,* IV, 407. 21 May 1793.

92. *Ibid.,* IV, 477. 8 Dec. 1793.

93. *Monthly Review* N.S. X (March 1793), 297–98.

94. *European Magazine* XXVIII (Nov. 1795), 324.

95. *Analytical Review* XXIV (1796), 398–99.

96. Joseph Priestley, *An Appeal to the Public on the Subject of the Riots in Birmingham,* Part II (London, 1792).

97. Birmingham Mss. 24 Jan. 1793.

98. Kegan Paul, *Godwin,* I, 263.

99. Birmingham Mss. 27 Sept. 1794.

100. Hutton, "Memoir" in *Monthly Magazine* XIII, 478.

101. The letter is simply dated 7 Dec. Scott dated it 1795, but it probably belongs to the earlier year. His version ("Prefatory Memoir," p. xxii) is considerably altered from the original, presumably by Catherine Hutton, in the interests of conventional English. Scott has "thou varlet" for "you monkey"; "does not smoke" for "don't smoke"; "overplus" for "Overplus." He also omits the sentence about the £20 wage increase, and ends the passage quite differently: "No matter. Ten years hence, perhaps, I shall not care a farthing." Perhaps the original ending was felt to be flippant; the one used is taken from a letter of 28 Nov. 1787. Scott has a footnote indicating that the "prophecy" was fulfilled with Bage's death a year later, and he would hardly have made this point had he been aware that the letter was not altogether genuine.

102. *Ibid.,* 4 July 1796.

103. *Ibid.*, 8 Sept. 1796; Scott, "Prefatory Memoir," p. xxii.

104. *Analytical Review* XXIV (1796), 608. *The Sincere Huron* was the title of F. Ashmore's 1786 translation of *L'Ingénu.*

105. *British Critic* VII (April 1796), 430.

106. *Monthly Review* XXI (September 1796), 21.

107. See Anthony Lincoln, *Political and Social Ideas of English Dissent, 1763–1800* (Cambridge, 1938), p. 35ff. for an account of the Dissenting influence on the press.

109. Kegan Paul, *Godwin,* I, 261. 15 June 1797.

110. *Ibid.,* I, 262.

111. *Ibid.*

112. *Ibid.,* I, 263. Holbach's *Système de la Nature* (1770) gave a materialist account of the universe and was widely known. Basil Willey discusses it in *Eighteenth Century Background* (London, 1950), Ch. IX, where Godwin is described as "the chief English exponent of Holbach's ideas"; p. 167.

113. Kegan Paul, *Godwin,* I, 264.

114. *Ibid.,* I, 267. 19 June 1797.

115. Birmingham Mss. Feb. 1797.

116. *Ibid.,* 21 Oct. 1799.

117. *Ibid.*

118. *Ibid.,* 27 March 1800.

119. *Ibid.,* 8 Jan. 1800; Scott, "Prefatory Memoir," p. xxiii, prints a tidied-up version dated March 1801.

120. Birmingham Mss. 11 March 1800.

121. Kegan Paul, *Godwin,* I, 262.

122. See Godwin's MS. journal, 1788–1834, in the Bodleian Library, Oxford.

123. Birmingham Mss. 24 Jan. 1801.

124. *Ibid.,* 26 March 1801.

125. Hutton, "Memoir" in *Monthly Magazine,* XIII, 480.

126. Hutton, *Life* (1816), pp. 239–40.

127. *Derby Mercury,* 10 Sept. 1801, p. 4.

Chapter Two

1. "Courtney Melmoth" (S. J. Pratt), *Shenstone-Green: or, the New Paradise Lost* (London, 1779). There is a good summary of this novel in J. M. S. Tompkins, *The Popular Novel in England 1770–1800* (1932). Reissue (London, 1961), 192–93. Miss Tompkins then goes on to a good discussion of Bage's novels.

2. William Shenstone, *Essays on Men and Manners* in *Works,* ed. R. Dodsley (London, 1768), II, 141–42.

3. Bage, *Mount Henneth. A Novel in a Series of Letters* (1782).

Quotations in this book are from the British Library copy, which is of the second edition (London, 1788). The text was slightly revised for Scott's edition of 1824 in *Ballantyne's Novelist's Library.*

4. Paul Hazard, *European Thought in the Eighteenth Century* (1946; English translation 1954) (London, 1965), pp. 187–88.

5. For the whole subject, see A. M. Lyles, *Methodism Mocked* (London, 1960). Curiously, however, this study contains no reference to Bage.

6. See H. N. Fairchild, *The Noble Savage* (Columbia, 1928), Ch. V. "Some English Jacobins." Dr. Fairchild refers to Lahontan's *Dialogues de Monsieur le Baron de Lahontan et d'un Sauvage* (1709) and Franklin's *Remarks Concerning the Savages of North America* (1784), in the context of a parallel scene in *Hermsprong* (1796). Fielding's Parson Adams in *Joseph Andrews* (1742), I, 17, also asserts that "a virtuous and good Turk, or Heathen, are more acceptable in the sight of their Creator, than a vicious and wicked Christian, though his faith were as perfectly orthodox as St. Paul himself."

7. Hazard, *European Thought,* pp. 128–29.

8. Scott's "Prefatory Memoir," p. xxx. Scott's attitude to Bage is considered in Ch. 1 and Ch. 8. Bage's feminism is discussed breezily in G. P. Utter and G. B. Needham, *Pamela's Daughters* (London, 1937). Mary Wollstonecraft's *Vindication of the Rights of Woman* appeared in 1792. She is referred to by Bage in *Hermsprong* (1796), and herself reviewed *Man as He Is,* anonymously, in the *Analytical Review* in the same year.

9. Heilman, *America in English Fiction,* pp. 56, 58.

10. Henry Mackenzie, *The Man of Feeling* (1771), ed. Brian Vickers (London, 1967), pp. 93–94.

11. Heilman, *America in English Fiction,* p. 98.

12. *Monthly Review,* LXVI (1782), 130; quoted by Heilman, *America in English Fiction,* p. 71.

13. See D. M. Clark, *British Opinion and the American Revolution* (1930). Reissue (New York, 1966), Ch. VI. "Activities and Views of the Radicals."

14. *Ibid.* Ch. IV. "The Mercantile Classics." 3. "During the War."

15. Presumably a reference to the debating society for ladies which enjoyed a brief vogue in London; see Wendeborn, *A View of England, I,* 252ff., which also describes Ranelagh and Vauxhall as striking features of London social life.

16. The Antiquarian Society was often made a butt for satire. Wendeborn defended the society, which was founded in 1757, and published its *Transactions* from 1770, noting that it was too severely criticized for dealing with "trifles, and the sweepings of antiquity." Wendeborn, *A View of England* II, 117. The next quotation given from the novel is also relevant. Antony van Leeuwenhoeck (1632–1723) was a celebrated Dutch microscopist who published numerous articles in the *Philosophical Transactions* of the Royal Society.

17. J. O. Bartley, *Teague, Shenkin and Sawney* (Cork, 1954), Ch. XIII. "The Stage Scotsman 1756–1800."

18. No observant man of the time was likely to be unaware of the cult of the picturesque and its effect on the English landscape, but there were three local manifestations of which Bage was particularly likely to be aware: Shenstone's famous *ferme ornée* at the Leasowes; Donegall's Fisherwick Park, already discussed (see Ch. I); and Erasmus Darwin's botanic garden near Lichfield, begun as recently as 1777 and described by Anna Seward thus:

It was irriguous from many springs, and swampy from their plentitude. In some parts he widened the brook into small lakes; in others, he taught it to wind between shrubby margins. Not only with trees of various growth did he adorn the borders of the fountain, but with various classes of plants, uniting the Linnean science with the charm of landscape.

Anna Seward, *Memoirs of the Life of Dr. Darwin* (London, 1804), pp. 125–27. For the general subject, see Christopher Hussey, *The Picturesque. Studies in a Point of View* (New York, 1927).

19. Alexander Cozens, *Principles of Beauty Relative to the Human Head* (London, 1778). I am indebted for this information to Mr. J. A. S. Ingamells of the Wallace Collection.

20. Laurence Sterne, *A Sentimental Journey through France and Italy* (1768), "The Gloves."

21. H. Fluchère, *Laurence Sterne: from Tristram to Yorick*. English translation and abridgment by Barbara Bray (1961) (Oxford, 1965), p. 392.

22. *Ibid.*, p. 363.

23. Scott, "Prefatory Memoir," p. xviii.

24. *Ibid.*, p. xxvi.

25. *Ibid.*

26. Tompkins, *Popular Novel,* p. 67.

27. F. C. Green, *Minuet* (London, 1935), p. 194.

28. By 1784, the following translations had been published: Of Voltaire: *Zadig* (1749); *Micromégas* (1753); *Babouc* (1754); *Candid* (1759) and *Candidus* (1759); *L'Ingénu: or the Sincere Huron* (1768); *The Pupil of Nature* (1771); *Young James* (1776). In addition, Smollett and Franklin published the *Works* in 25 vols. (1761–65) and in 38 vols. (1778–81). Kenrick and Downman also produced the *Works* in 14 vols. (1779–81). Of Rousseau: *Eloisa* (1761); *Emilius and Sophia* (1762); *Emilius* (1763). See *New Cambridge Bibliography of English Literature, II, 1660–1800* (Cambridge, 1971), 99–102; 97, 143.

29. H. Roddier, *J. J. Rousseau en Angleterre au XVIII siècle* (Paris, 1950), p. 361.

Chapter Three

1. Bage, *Barham Downs. A Novel* (London, 1784). Quotations are from the British Library copy of the first edition.
2. A. R. Humphreys, *William Shenstone. An Eighteenth Century Portrait* (London, 1937), 12.
3. Samuel Richardson, *The History of Clarissa Harlowe* (1747–48), IV. Letter CV (London, 1962), IV, 304.
4. A. D. McKillop, *Samuel Richardson, Printer and Novelist* (1936) (North Carolina, 1960), p. 241.
5. *Ibid.*
6. Lucy Strode exhibits exactly the combination of "sensibility" and prudence which Fielding so disliked in Richardson's Pamela. Sir George later gives a nicely ironical description of the scene which ended his proposal:

Panting with sensibility, her virtue was every now and then ready to give up the ghost; constantly, at the dying minute she recovered to a sense of honour. It is true she almost reverenced my profound wisdom, and vast abilities, but chastity was dearer to her than life. My profound wisdom fell into the snare, and I married her the next morning.

7. Bage probably had in mind Price's *Observations on the Nature of Civil Liberty* (1776), which argued that government existed for the good of the people, and that a more representative parliament was necessary for progress and as a guarantee of liberty. William Eden (later Lord Auckland) was one of the five Commissioners sent to America in 1778. His *Four Letters to the Earl of Carlisle* (1779) had reached a third edition by 1780. In the first letter Eden criticized those who "wrest every observation to prove, that their own country is, and in the nature of things ought to be, ruined" (Eden, *Four Letters to the Earl of Carlisle,* third edition [London, 1780], 8). But he also criticized extravagant optimists. In letter five (added to the third edition), he contrasted the "civil liberty" of "freer nations" with conditions in France and other absolute monarchies (*Four Letters,* 181).
8. See E. C. Black, *The Association* (Cambridge, Mass., 1963), Chs. II and III.
9. See R. W. Harris, *Political Ideas 1760–1792* (London, 1963), Ch. VIII, "William Pitt and the Business of Government"; Clark, *British Opinion,* Ch. VIII, "The Influence of the Crown."
10. Scott, "Prefatory Memoir," p. xxx.
11. See A. Lincoln, *Some Political & Social Ideas of English Dissent 1763–1800* (London, 1938), Ch. VI, "Toleration and the Rights of Man, Citizens and Christians"; and U. R. Q. Henriques, *Religious Toleration in England 1787–1833* (London, 1961).

12. See R. R. Fennessy, *Burke, Paine and the Rights of Man* (The Hague, 1963), pp. 56ff.

13. Foner (ed.), *Paine* (II), 285.

14. *Ibid.* (I), 464.

15. Priestley (ed.), *Political Justice* II, 213ff.

16. For the characterization of the stage Irishman see J. O. Bartley, *Teague, Shenkin and Sawney,* Ch. X.

17. F. C. Green, *Jean-Jacques Rousseau: A Critical Study* (London, 1955), p. 208.

18. L. Whitney, *Primitivism and the Idea of Progress in English Popular Literature of the Eighteenth Century* (Baltimore, 1934), p. 270.

Chapter Four

1. *Monthly Review* LXXVI (April 1787), 325–29; see Ch. I.

2. Osborne, "Bibliography," 31.

3. My quotations are from a microfilm of the 1787 Dublin pirated edition kindly supplied by the Bibliothèque Nationale in Paris. The rarity of the novel explains the fact that Heilman, *America in English Fiction,* 83 and 147, knew it only through a review, so that his comments on it are inaccurate. Bage already appears prominently in Heilman's book, and *The Fair Syrian* would entitle him to an even larger place.

4. J. R. Foster, *History of the Pre-Romantic Novel in England* (New York, 1949), pp. 233–34.

5. H. R. Steeves, *Before Jane Austen* (London, 1966), p. 277.

6. This is a pun on the title of Paine's famous pamphlet, *Common-Sense* (1776), which did so much to strengthen American resistance to English demands. Paine actually landed in Philadelphia, where the strength of the Quaker community was well known.

7. See Swift, *Gulliver's Travels,* Book II, "A Voyage to Brobdingnag"; it is the opinion of the King of Brobdingnag.

8. Joseph and Etienne Montgolfier made the first successful public trial at Annonay on 5 June 1783. Balloons rapidly became a vogue in both France and England. In England Lunardi made several spectacular flights in 1784; a crowd at Moorfield in September saw him rise four miles. In January 1785 John Jeffries and J. P. Blanchard crossed the Channel by balloon. See A. Wolf, *A History of Science, Technology and Philosophy in the Eighteenth Century* (1938); second edition, revised by D. McKie (London, 1952), pp. 577–78.

9. See M. P. Constant, *The Oriental Tale in England in the Eighteenth Century* (1908); New York, 1966): *The Fair Syrian* is dismissed on p. 51 as "a long and tedious novel."

10. See H. Roddier, *L'Abbé Prévost* (Paris, 1955), pp. 138–39.

11. Steeves, *Before Jane Austen,* p. 280.

12. See Tompkins, *Popular Novel*, p. 205: "It is impossible to read in *The Fair Syrian* the Georgian Amine's account of her slavery without thinking of Voltaire." Dr. Tompkins had read the novel in French translation (hence the spelling Amine), but comments: "The translation naturally emphasises the likeness, but does not account for it" (*ibid.*, p. 205, footnote).

13. T. Paine, *The Rights of Man,* edited by H. Collins (Harmondsworth, 1969), p. 102.

Chapter Five

1. Bage, *James Wallace,* 3 vols. (London, 1788). Quotations are from the (imperfect) British Library copy of the first edition.

2. See Ch. I.

3. Crébillon was regarded in England as an immoral novelist; see, for example, an ironical reference in the *Gentleman's Magazine* in 1784: "His works have been responsible for the foundation of some of the most recent, and the most remarkable divorces that ever took place." *Gentleman's Magazine XIV* (1784), I, 391.

4. See John Moore, *Mordaunt,* ed. W. L. Renwick (London, 1965), Letter 117. In his Introduction, p. xiv, Professor Renwick remarks of the novelists of the period: "Only Robert Bage belonged, with Moore, to Fielding's world." He prefers Moore as the more realistic, less didactic novelist. In this case, however, it is Bage who is the realist.

5. Foster, *Pre-Romantic Novel,* p. 2.

6. Thomas R. Preston, *The Good-Natured Misanthrope: A Study in the Satire and Sentiment of the Eighteenth Century.* Unpublished doctoral dissertation (Rice University, 1962). Quoted by R. Paulson, *Satire and the Novel in Eighteenth Century England* (Yale, 1967), p. 218.

7. T. R. Preston, "Smollett and the Benevolent Misanthrope," *P.M.L.A.* LXXIX (1964), 57.

8. Paulson, *Satire and the Novel,* p. 245.

9. Voltaire's *Zadig* (1747) was translated into English as early as 1749, as *Zadig: or, the Book of Fate* and again in 1780; see *New Cambridge Bibliography,* ed. G. Watson, II, 99–100. Wallace's last quoted remark also has a literary origin, in a well-known couplet of Pope: "Let humble Allen, with an awkward shame, / Do good by stealth, and blush to find it fame." Pope, "Epilogue to the Satires," Dialogue 1, lines 135–36.

10. The quotation is again from Pope; *An Essay on Man,* Epistle IV, lines 203–204.

11. Scott, "Prefatory Memoir," p. xxxiv.

12. See Pierre Vitoux's unpublished doctoral dissertation of 1964 on Bage for the University of Paris. Some remarks in Priestley's *History and Present State of Electricity* (1767) are quoted, including the statement that

"the growth of vegetables is quickened by electricity" (Priestley, *History,* third edition [1775], II, 6). Vitoux also refers to the satirical novel, *The Philosophical Quixote: or, the Memoirs of Mr. David Wilkins* (1782) in which a country apothecary tries to apply science to medicine, and hopes, by charging people with electricity, to enable them to repel raindrops. See Tompkins, *Popular Novel,* p. 190.

13. Paracelsus (1491–1541) was the best-known medieval scientist.

14. Glass was a Midland industry in which several members of the Lunar Society were interested. Keir (referred to by Bage in *Man as He Is* in 1792) was manager of a Stourbridge glassworks, and there is an undated reference in James Watt's Common Place Book I, "some thoughts upon the improvement of Flint glass for optical purposes," which refers to conversations with "friend Keir." Experiments are recorded for March and April 1783. See Schofield, *Lunar Society,* pp. 81, 172.

15. Lazzare Spalanzani (1729–1799) was an Italian abbot and professor of physiology, noted as an opponent of the idea of spontaneous generation; see Wolf, *History of Science,* pp. 471, 474.

16. Wendeborn, *A View of England,* II, 110.

17. There are specific references to Lord Chesterfield's well-known view that laughter was ill-bred by Paracelsus Holman (I, 103) and Miss Thurl (II, 66).

18. Hazard, *European Thought,* p. 147.

19. *Ibid.,* p. 230.

20. A. R. Humphreys, *The Augustan World* (London, 1954), p. 84.

21. *Ibid.,* p. 89.

22. G. F. Singer, *The Epistolary Novel* (1932); reissue (New York, 1965), pp. 125–26. *The Fair Syrian* is particularly praised for this.

23. *Ibid.,* p. 125.

24. F. G. Black, *The Epistolary Novel in the Late Eighteenth Century* (Eugene, 1940), Ch. II, "1791–1800." Black also remarks that "letters are sentimental documents"; *Ibid.,* p. 108.

Chapter Six

1. See *New Cambridge Bibliography,* ed. G. Watson, II, 843, 1101, 1249.

2. William Hazlitt, "My First Acquaintance with Poets," in *Works,* Centenary Edition, ed. P. P. Howe, XVII (London, 1933), 122.

3. *Man as He Is* (London, 1792). Preface, i–iii. Quotations from the British Library copy. The reference is to Rousseau's second Preface to *La Nouvelle Héloise* (1761), entitled "Dialogue entre un Homme de lettres et J. J. Rousseau." Rousseau argues that the novel will exert a moral influence, especially on female readers who would avoid more serious readings. See H. Roddier, *J. J. Rousseau en Angleterre en XVIII Siècle* (Paris, 1949), p. 73.

4. II, 158. Louis Weltjie died in 1800 having become Clerk of the Kitchen to the Prince of Wales. He kept, according to his obituary notice, "one of the most fashionable taverns in the metropolis, which was the resort of the highest of our nobility." *Gentleman's Magazine,* LXX (1800), 1109. Bage goes unconventionally far in admitting, if coyly, that his hero sometimes visited prostitutes in referring to Mrs. Sinclair, the brothel-keeper in Richardson's *Clarissa.*

5. The characterization of Mr. Bardoe may derive from a suggestion in Dr. John Moore's *A View of Society and Manners in Italy* (London, 1781), to which Bage refers in his account of Italy. Moore contrasts the liveliness of the Italians at an opera with the affected *nonchalance* of some English gentlemen and their imitators:

Those who wish to be thought of what is called *ton,* imitate the mawkish insipidity of their superiors in rank, and imagine it distinguishes them from the vulgar, to suppress all the natural expressions of pity, joy, or admiration, and to seem, upon all occasions, in a state of complete apathy.

Moore, *A View,* II, 198.

6. The danger of Italy to the ill-informed English art collector was well known. Wendeborn — *A View of England,* II, 186 — comments sensibly:

In my opinion, those who send these sums to Italy, would do better to apply at least a part of them, as an encouragement for their own fellow-countrymen, who discover a genius for the fine arts, instead of giving so much money to Italian painters, who, besides, impose too frequently upon the ignorant, by selling copies only instead of originals.

It is a twist of Bage's, however, that the dealer here should be a Scot.

7. For Bage's attitude to Burke, see also pp. 119-20 above.

8. Osborne, "Bibliography," pp. 33-34.

9. *The British Novelists,* ed. Mrs. Barbauld, XLVIII, *Man as He Is Not; or Hermsprong* (London, 1810), Preface, ii-iii.

10. Tompkins, *Popular Novel,* p. 196.

11. Steeves, *Before Jane Austen,* p. 282.

12. See Wendeborn, *A View of England,* I, 288: "The host of these mercenaries of the Cyprian goddess have been reckoned to be in London stronger than forty thousand."

13. Leibnitz (1646-1716) and Malebranche (1638-1715) were two of the great Rationalist system-builders. Later Bage refers to the optimism of Leibnitz, in the spirit of Voltaire's *Candide* (1759): "Everything in the world is the best possible. Leibnitz taught this grave truth, and everybody believes it — but the unhappy" (IV, 170).

14. Dr. Thomas Reid was the best-known philosopher of the Scottish "common-sense" school, which was probably sympathetic to Bage. Reid's *Essay on the Intellectual Powers of Man* appeared in 1785 and was one of

the books borrowed by Bage from the library of the Derby Philosophical Society in 1789.

15. Robert Young, *An Essay on the Powers and Mechanism of Nature* (London, 1788), p. xi.

16. F. J. Copleston, *A History of Philosophy,* VI (London, 1960), 118–19.

17. John Moore, *A View of Society and Manners in Italy* (London, 1781), I, 338, gives a sardonic account of the belief that Mary's house flew across from Nazareth to avoid the Turkish invasions, and eventually settled at Loretto. He also criticizes those Christians who "condemn their fellow creatures to cruel deaths for speculative opinions," who think it their duty "to spend their whole lives in cells, doing nothing," and who weave around the simple truths of Christianity "mysterious webs of various texture" (*ibid.,* I, 360–61).

18. See J. M. Holzman, *The Nabobs in England. A Study of the Returned Anglo-Indian, 1760–1785* (New York, 1926), 23–24:

When the Nabob returned to his own country, he found the social rank assigned him even more unaccustomed and unpleasant, than the graces which he had forgotten. . . . Naturally, he revolted; bad temper was joined to bad manners.

19. L. Whitney, *Primitivism and the Idea of Progress in English Popular Literature of the Eighteenth Century* (Baltimore, 1934), Ch. 2, "Simplicity Versus Luxury and Degeneration."

20. J. A. de Luc, *Lettres physiques et morales sur les montagnes,* 6 vols. (La Haye, 1778–80). De Luc was a pious Swiss geologist who tried to reconcile Genesis with his studies. He settled in England in 1773, later being an F. R. S. Reader to Queen Charlotte, to whom the book is dedicated. De Luc visited the Soho works in 1782, and did some experiments with James Watt. Schofield, *Lunar Society,* p. 240.

21. For Madan, see *Dictionary of National Biography* XXV (London, 1893), 289–90. The full title of his work was *Thelyphthora; a Treatise on female ruin in its causes, effects, consequences, prevention and remedy* (London, 1780).

22. In 1792 over five hundred petitions were presented to Parliament in support of Wilberforce's third bill for abolition. The bill was delayed by the Lords, and the growth of antiradical feeling during the French wars led to a delay of some fifteen years before abolition was finally achieved; see D. Read, *The English Provinces* (London, 1964), p. 42.

23. Lafayette (1757–1834) was the French hero of the American War of Independence, and Lally-Tollendal (1751–1830) was another prominent liberal-minded aristocrat.

24. See W. L. Renwick, *English Literature 1789–1815* (London, 1963), Ch. II, "The Destiny of Nations," esp. pp. 19–25.

25. IV, 71–72. In December 1790 Burke was awarded an honorary L.L.D.

by Trinity College, Dublin. According to Magnus: "An attempt was made to confer a similar honour upon him at Oxford, but it was feared that convocation would not be unanimous." Sir Philip Magnus, *Edmund Burke — A Life* (London, 1939), p. 211.

26. IV, 72; see Burke, *Reflections on the Revolution in France* (1790), in *Works* (London, 1828), III, 331.

27. See "Preface," note 11, and 7 above.

28. Schofield, *Lunar Society*, p. 27.

29. II, 219-20. For some discussion of the Lunar Society of which Boulton, Priestley, Keir and Darwin were members, see Ch. 1 above.

Chapter Seven

1. *Hermsprong: or Man as He Is Not* (1796). Quotations are from the British Library copy of the 1796 Dublin pirated edition.

2. Wayne C. Booth, *The Rhetoric of Fiction* (Chicago, 1961), p. 235. Booth contrasts the success of Diderot and Bage with the failure of Mackenzie in *The Man of Feeling* (1771) to give new life to the Shandean mode.

3. Fairchild, *Noble Savage*, esp. Ch. V, "Some English Jacobins."

4. English translations of *L'Ingénu* appeared in 1768, 1771, and 1786. Quotations are from the anonymous translation, *The Pupil of Nature: a True History* (London, 1771).

5. J. R. Foster, *History of the Pre-Romantic Novel in England* (New York, 1949), p. 237, draws elaborate parallels between the two novels.

6. III, 18. A similar motive impels Higgs in his efforts among the Erewhonians in Samuel Butler's *Erewhon* (1872) (London, 1962), p. 30.

7. Bissell, *American Indian* 75, suggests that Bage may have derived it from a passage in Franklin's *Remarks concerning the Savages of North America* (1784), in *Two Tracts* (London, 1784), pp. 31-33.

8. Dr. Samuel Horsley (1733-1806), Bishop and F. R. S., was noted for his controversial writings against Priestley. According to the *Dictionary of National Biography:* "On 30th Jan. 1793 he preached a remarkable sermon before the House of Lords at Westminster Abbey, depicting the danger of the revolutionary spirit: as he began his peroration the whole assembly rose in rapt enthusiasm." *Dictionary of National Biography,* XXVII, 384.

9. See *Man as He Is,* I, 253, and Ch. VI, Note 21.

10. Charles P. Moritz, *Travels, Chiefly on foot, in 1782* (English translation, 1795) ed. P. E. Matheson (London, 1924), p. 110.

11. Blakey, *Minerva Press,* p. 65. Another comparable pair are Mr. and Mrs. Darnley in John Moore's *Mordaunt* (1800).

12. P. Vitoux, *Robert Bage* (unpublished dissertation for the University of Paris, 1964), Ch. VII.

13. Perhaps the new edition of *Hermsprong* for the Oxford English Novels series will throw some light, at least on the italics. It is pertinent to observe that the ending of Mrs. Inchbald's *Nature and Art,* also of 1796, strikes a quietist note.

14. Three prominent liberal writers: Sir James Mackintosh (1765–1832) replied to Burke's *Reflections* in *Vindiciae Gallicae* (1791); Thomas Christie (1761–1796) in *Letters on the Revolution in France and the New Constitution established by the National Assembly* (1791); and Benjamin Flower (1755–1829) also published a defense of the French Constitution (1792), as well as editing the *Cambridge Intelligencer,* which opposed the war with France.

15. James Francis Edward Keith, commonly known as Marshal Keith (1696–1758), was the greatest of all the "Scots abroad," serving Russia, and then Prussia, throughout the first part of the Seven Years War, being killed at the battle of Hochkirsh.

16. See Professor Dobrée's remarks on the prominence of *banditti* in Mrs. Radcliffe's novels: "*banditti* — a type of confederation essential to her novels — her Sicily abounded with them." *The Mysteries of Udolpho,* edited by B. Dobrée (London, 1966), Introduction, p. X.

17. Osborne, "Bibliography," p. 36.

18. Walter Allen, *The English Novel* (Harmondsworth, 1958), p. 102.

19. Tompkins, *Popular Novel,* p. 198.

20. J. H. Sutherland, "Robert Bage: Novelist of Ideas," in *Philological Quarterly* XXXVI (1957), 211.

21. *Ibid.,* 220.

22. *Hermsprong,* edited by Vaughan Wilkins (London, 1957), Introduction, p. viii.

Chapter Eight

1. See Osborne, "Bibliography," p. 31.

2. Quoted by E. P. Thompson, *English Working Class,* p. 495.

3. *The British Novelists,* ed. Mrs. Barbauld, XLVIII, *Man as He Is Not; or Hermsprong* (London, 1810), pp. 1–2.

4. *Ibid.,* p. 3.

5. *Ibid.*

6. M. Jaeger, *Before Victoria, Changing Standards of Behaviour 1787–1837* (1956). Penguin edition (Harmondsworth, 1967), p. 81.

7. Lord Mahon, *History of England 1713–83.* Third edition (London, 1854), VII, 324.

8. *Ibid.,* p. 326.

9. *The Life of Mary Ann Schimmelpenninck,* ed. C. C. Hankin, I (London, 1858), 125.

10. *Ibid.,* I, 126. Lockhart's account of Scott's reasons for not continu-

ing with the *Novelist's Library* after Ballantyne's death in 1822 is relevant. Scott argued that no such collection could be successful, since it would contain "a large proportion of matter, condemned by the purity, whether real or affected, of modern taste." Lockhart remarks that this purity may be seen in Scott's own novels, "in which no purist could pretend to discover danger for the morals of youth." Lockhart, *Life of Scott,* VI, 271.

11. Scott, "Prefatory Memoir," pp. xxv–xxvi. The "Memoir" is now also available in *Sir Walter Scott on Novelists and Fiction,* ed. I. Williams (London, 1968).

12. *Ibid.,* p. xxvi.

13. *Ibid.*

14. *Ibid.*

15. *Ibid.*

16. *Ibid.*

17. *Ibid.,* p. xxvii.

18. *Ibid.,* p. xxviii.

19. *Ibid.,* p. xxix.

20. *Ibid.*

21. *Ibid.,* p. xxx.

22. *Ibid.*

23. *Ibid.* See my article, "Scott as Editor of Bage," in *Notes and Queries* XVII, 10 (Oct. 1970), 376–78, for evidence that editorial interference was in fact minimal.

24. *Ibid.,* p. xxxi.

25. *Ibid.,* p. xxxii.

26. *Ibid.,* p. xxxiii.

27. *Ibid.,* p. xxxiv.

28. *Ibid.*

29. *Ibid.*

30. *Ibid.*

31. Scott, *Lives of the Novelists* (London, 1928), Introduction, p. ix.

32. *Quarterly Review,* XXXIV (Sept. 1826), 367.

33. *Ibid.,* p. 370.

34. *Henry Crabb Robinson on Books and their Writers,* ed. E. J. Morley, 2 vols. (London, 1938), I, 319.

35. Rev. A. G. L'Estrange, *The Life of Mary Russell Mitford,* second edition (London, 1870), III, 299–300 (Dec. 1854).

36. M. Jaeger, *Before Victoria,* p. 124.

37. *The Reliquary. Quarterly Archaeological Journal and Review* X (1869–70), 37.

38. *Dictionary of National Biography* II (London, 1885), 391–93.

39. H. R. Steeves, *Before Jane Austen* (London, 1966), p. 291.

40. Aldous Huxley, *Point Counter Point* (1928) (Harmondsworth, 1955), p. 299.

41. *Hermsprong,* ed. Vaughan Wilkins (London, 1951), Introduction,

p. v.

42. J. H. Sutherland, "Robert Bage: Novelist of Ideas" in *Philological Quarterly,* 36 (1957), 211.

43. Walter Allen, *The English Novel* (1954) (London, 1958), p. 102.

44. See Stuart Piggott, "The Roman Camp in Three Authors," *Review of English Literature* VII, 3 (July 1966), 25.

45. H. Mills, *Peacock, His Circle and His Age* (Cambridge, 1969), p. 84.

46. *Mary Shelley's Journal,* ed. F. L. Jones (Norman, OK, 1947), p. 43.

Selected Bibliography

PRIMARY SOURCES

1. Novels

Mount Henneth. London: T. Lowndes, 1782.
Barham Downs. London: G. Wilkie, 1784.
The Fair Syrian. London: J. Walter, 1787.
James Wallace. London: William Lane, The Minerva Press, 1788.
Man as He Is Not. London: William Lane, The Minerva Press, 1792.
Hermsprong, or Man as He Is Not. London: The Minerva Press, 1796.

2. Letters

The Letters of Robert Bage, Paper-Maker of Elford and Later Resident at Tamworth, to William Hutton of Birmingham 1782–1801. In the Birmingham Public Library, Local Studies Library. Mss. 486802.
Extracts also in the Hutton-Beale Collection, no. 29 A-C, in the same Library.

SECONDARY SOURCES

1. Bibliography

OSBORNE, E. A. "A Preliminary Survey for a Bibliography of the Novels of Robert Bage," in *Book Handbook,* edited by R. Horrox. Bracknell, Berkshire, 1951.
WATSON, GEORGE, editor. *The New Cambridge Bibliography of English Literature, II, 1660–1800,* Cambridge: University Press, 1971.

2. Early Criticism and Background Material

BARBAULD, MRS. ANNE. "Preface, biographical and critical" to *Man as He Is Not; or Hermsprong* in *The British Novelists,* XLVIII. London: F. C. and J. Rivington, 1810. The earliest critical summary of Bage's achievement.
HOLCROFT, THOMAS. Review of *Man as He Is* in *Monthly Review* X (March 1793), 297–302. By a contemporary radical novelist.
HUTTON, WILLIAM. *The Life of William Hutton; including a particular account of the Riots at Birmingham in 1791.* London: J. Nichols and

Son, 1816. The work of Bage's friend and correspondent.

_____. *An History of Birmingham to the End of the Year 1780.* Birmingham: T. Pearson, 1781. Valuable background information.

_____. *The History of Derby to the Year 1791.* London: J. and J. Robinson, 1791. Contains Hutton's tribute to Bage.

KEIR, JAMES. *An Account of the Life and Writings of Thomas Day, Esq.* London: J. Stockdale, 1791. Contains many striking parallels of outlook and attitude with Bage.

SCOTT, WALTER. "Prefatory Memoir to Bage" in *Ballantyne's Novelist's Library, IX, Novels of Swift, Bage and Cumberland.* London: Hurst, Robinson and Co., 1824. The fullest early account of Bage and his achievement.

TAYLOR, WILLIAM. Review of *Hermsprong* in *Monthly Review* XXI (September 1796), 21–24. A sympathetic response.

WENDEBORN, G. F. A. *A View of England towards the Close of the Eighteenth Century,* 2 vols. London: G. G. J. and J. Robinson, 1791. Originally written in German, the book gives a clear account of the state of England at the time.

WOLLSTONECRAFT, MARY. Review of *Man as He Is* in *Analytical Review* XXIV (October 1796), 398–99. A review by the feminist writer.

3. Recent Criticism and Background Material

BAKER, ERNEST A. *The History of the English Novel,* V. London: H. F. and G. Witherby, 1934. An American scholar who sees Bage as typically English in his moderate approach to social problems.

BLACK, FRANK G. *The Epistolary Novel in the Late Eighteenth Century.* Eugene: University of Oregon, 1940. A thorough study of the decline of the convention, with a favorable account of Bage.

BLAKEY, DOROTHY. *The Minerva Press 1790–1820.* Oxford: the Bibliographical Society, 1939. A very thorough study, with a sympathetic section on Bage as a Minerva Press novelist.

BOULTON, JAMES T. *The Language of Politics in the Age of Wilkes and Burke.* London: Routledge and Kegan Paul; Toronto: University Press, 1963. A thorough and thoughtful account of the political controversies of the period in literary terms.

BUTLER, MARILYN. *Jane Austen and the War of Ideas.* Oxford: The Clarendon Press, 1975. A good account of *Hermsprung* in its context.

COBBAN, ALFRED, editor. *The Debate on the French Revolution 1789–1800.* London: Nicholas Kaye, 1950.

CROSS, WILBUR L. *Development of the English Novel.* New York: Macmillan Co., 1899. Discusses Bage in a thoughtful chapter on "The Novel of Purpose."

DOWDEN, EDWARD. *The French Revolution and English Literature.* London: Kegan Paul and Co., 1897. The earliest treatment of the subject, it seems to derive the account of Bage largely from Scott.

don: Edward Arnold, 1912. A lively but rather condescending placing of Bage in his period.

FAIRCHILD, HOXIE NEALE. *The Noble Savage: A Study in Romantic Naturalism.* New York: Columbia University Press, 1928. A thorough survey of this important theme, making exhaustive suggestions about possible influences shaping *Hermsprong.*

FOSTER, JAMES R. *History of the Pre-Romantic Novel in England.* New York: Modern Languages Association of America; London: Oxford University Press, 1949. Places Bage well in context in a chapter called "Liberal Opinions," describing him interestingly as "the sentimental Smollett."

GALE, W. K. V. *Boulton, Watt and the Soho Undertakings.* Birmingham: Department of Science and Industry, 1952. Contains valuable information about the factory referred to by Bage in *Man as He Is.*

GILL, CONRAD. *History of Birmingham,* I. London: Oxford University Press, 1952. Authoritative and lucid historical work.

GRABO, CARL H. "Robert Bage: A Forgotten Novelist," in *Mid-West Quarterly,* V, 3 (April 1918), 202–26. A lively plea for Bage.

GREGORY, ALLENE. *The French Revolution and the English Novel.* London and New York: G. P. Putnam's Sons, 1915. The most thoughtful early study, placing Bage well in his context.

HAZARD, PAUL. *European Thought in the Eighteenth Century.* Translated by J. Lewis May. London: Miller and Carter, 1965. A brilliant and wide-ranging discussion which provides a good background for understanding Bage's attitudes.

HEILMAN, ROBERT B. *America in English Fiction 1760–1800.* Baton Rouge: Louisiana State University Press, 1937. A careful consideration of the topic, though in the case of Bage, weakened by the lack of treatment of *The Fair Syrian* (then unobtainable).

HUMPHREYS, ARTHUR R. *The Augustan World. Life and Letters in Eighteenth-Century England.* London: Methuen and Co., 1954. A clear and thorough background book.

KEGAN PAUL, CHARLES, editor. *William Godwin. His Friends and Contemporaries,* 2 vols. London: Kegan Paul and Co., 1876. Contains Godwin's letters recording his visit to Bage in 1797.

KELLY, GARY. *The English Jacobin Novel 1780–1805.* Oxford: Clarendon Press, 1976. Scholarly study of four novelists, Bage, Godwin, Holcroft, and Mrs. Inchbald.

LINCOLN, ANTHONY. *Some Political and Social Ideas of English Dissent 1763–1800.* Cambridge: University Press, 1938. Helps to clarify the background of ideas.

MACCOBY, SIMON. *English Radicalism 1786–1832. From Paine to Cobbett.* London: Nicholas Kaye, 1955. Shows the varieties of Radicalism during Bage's period.

PRIESTLEY, F. E. L. Editor, William Godwin. *Enquiry Concerning Politi-*

cal Justice, 3 vols. Toronto: University Press, 1946. The most thorough exposition of late eighteenth-century Radical attitudes; finely edited.

RALEIGH, WALTER. *The English Novel.* London: Murray,1894. The first historical treatment of Bage, relating him to Rousseau but condescendingly amused at his social outlook.

RAMSDEN, HERMIONE. "Robert Bage: A Forgotten Novelist" in *The Yellow Book* XII (January 1897), 291–305. A thoughtful if slightly mannered plea for Bage.

RENWICK, WILLIAM L. *Oxford History of English Literature, IX, English Literature 1789–1815.* London: Oxford University Press, 1963. Argues that Bage's desire to get a message across prevents his novels from achieving a free sense of life.

SAINTSBURY, GEORGE. *The English Novel.* London: Dent, 1913. The first account to emphasize Bage's resemblance to French writers.

————. *The Peace of the Augustans.* London: G. Bell and Sons, 1916. Basically sympathetic but condescending in tone.

————. *Cambridge History of English Literature, XI, The Period of the French Revolution.* Cambridge: University Press, 1932. In this account, the emphasis falls on "fiction . . . succumbing to purpose."

SCHOFIELD, ROBERT E. *The Lunar Society of Birmingham.* London: Oxford University Press, 1963. A very thorough study of an important intellectual group.

SINGER, GODFREY F. *The Epistolary Novel.* Philadelphia: University of Pennsylvania Press, 1933. A wide-ranging study, which gives credit to Bage for his use of the convention.

STEEVES, HARRISON R. *Before Jane Austen.* London: Allen and Unwin, 1966. A pleasantly informed account of the early novel, devoting a whole chapter to Bage as "an eighteenth-century Shaw," but not overdoing the comparison.

SUTHERLAND, J. H. "Robert Bage: Novelist of Ideas," in *Philological Quarterly* XXXVI (1957). Sutherland wrote a thesis on Bage; in this article he drew a thoughtful distinction between the novel of ideas and the novel of doctrine, placing Bage's work in the first category.

TOMPKINS, J. M. S. *The Popular Novel in England 1770–1800.* London: Constable and Co., 1932. A thorough and lucid account of the subject, with a good section on Bage.

WHITNEY, LOIS. *Primitivism and the Idea of Progress in English Popular Fiction of the Eighteenth Century.* Baltimore: John Hopkins Press, 1934. Pays attention to Bage in this context, but does not allow for the flexibility of the novel in the discussion of social issues.

WILKINS, VAUGHAN. Introduction to *Hermsprong.* London: Turnstile Press, 1951. An enthusiastic and well-informed discussion of the novel.

WRIGHT, WALTER F. *Sensibility in English Prose Fiction 1760–1814.*

Urbana: University of Illinois Press, 1937. Rather oversystematized, but makes the valid point that Bage's social criticism contains both rational and emotional elements.

Index